IMAGES
of Sport

LEYTON ORIENT
FOOTBALL CLUB

Terry Mancini holds aloft the Division Three trophy in April 1970.

IMAGES
of Sport

LEYTON ORIENT
FOOTBALL CLUB

Compiled by
Neilson N. Kaufman

*This book is dedicated to my mother, Millie Kaufman and my father,
Zalic 'Sid' Kaufman; it was he who first planted the seed, back in 1957,
that led to my interest and search to ascertain the truth about the early
history of the club.*

TEMPUS

First published 2001
Copyright © Neilson N. Kaufman, 2001

Tempus Publishing Limited
The Mill, Brimscombe Port,
Stroud, Gloucestershire, GL5 2QG

ISBN 0 7524 2094 1

Typesetting and origination by
Tempus Publishing Limited
Printed in Great Britain by
Midway Clark Printing, Wiltshire

Regretfully, none of the images in this book are available for reproduction.

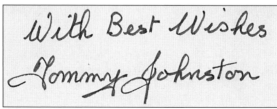

Tommy Johnston, the O's leading goalscorer, at his home in Australia with two tankards, presented by the club.

Contents

Foreword
by Barry Hearn

When I took over the ownership and running of Leyton Orient back in March 1995 – was it really so long ago? – one of the first things that became apparent to me was the deep-seated affection felt for the Orient by everyone involved with the club.

This included everyone from directors to supporters, from players to office staff, despite the fact that the club was going through a very tough time. I could see that Leyton Orient had the potential not only to achieve success on the field but to maintain and improve its standing as one of football's very few true family clubs.

Over the intervening five years a lot has changed at Brisbane Road. Development has got underway and the new South Stand is only the beginning of what is a long-term plan to turn the Matchroom Stadium into a twenty-first century football venue. This will take time but the recent purchase of a long-term lease means that the club has the kind of security that was a pipe-dream five years ago.

The finances of the club have been turned around and, while we are not rich by any stretch of the imagination, we can pay our milk bill, something the club was unable to do in the dark days of 1995. Football is a highly unusual business, and with so many small clubs currently a hair's breadth from receivership it is heartening to know that the O's are run in a properly business-like manner, which will preclude the kind of financial crisis endemic within the Football League.

On the playing side, things are starting to look up. I said when I first started at Brisbane Road that the long-term goal was to have a team made up of predominantly local kids who had made it through our youth development operation. That dream is well on the way to becoming a reality now, as this season our first team squad of twenty-seven players contains ten lads who have come through our youth system. That is very encouraging news indeed, and something which we will be building upon over the coming seasons.

I am a firm believer in spending money on young players, as £50,000 invested in local youth will yield far more value for Orient than a similar amount spent on one player who may only be with us for a season or two, with no guarantees whatsoever. Leyton Orient are very lucky to have Paul Brush, Peter Johnson and Martin Ling at the helm of its youth policy. They are tireless workers in this field and the type of coaches who are the envy of clubs far larger than us. Tommy Taylor continues to run the football side at Brisbane Road, and my faith and confidence in him is unwavering. Tom is an Orient man through and through and I'm sure that the success we hinted at in 1998/99 is something which we can look forward to in the very near future.

Over the last century many diverse characters have contributed to the continuing success of this great club, and we all owe a debt of gratitude to Neilson N. Kaufman, the club's Official Historian. He has put together this magnificent pictorial tribute to the life and times of of London's second oldest Football League club, so take great pleasure in this book, and here's to another 120 years of football at Brisbane Road.

Barry Hearn
Chairman, Leyton Orient FC

Introduction and Acknowledgements

First and foremost, I give thanks to ALL MIGHTY GOD for giving me this opportunity to finish this book after months of delays due to ill health and for the opportunity of making so many new friends and re-kindling old friendships. I am grateful that Tempus Publishing have given me the opportunity to add the story of the O's to their wonderful *Images of Sport* series. I would also like to thank Leyton Orient Football Club and in particular chairman and owner Barry Hearn for his full endorsement of this work and for the help of former club secretary Frank Woolf, assistant commercial manager Lynne Newman, Janet Hasler, Luke Riches at Matchroom Sports, my secretary Bianca van der Wath, John Munday and David Dodd, director of Leyton Orient.

I could not have completed this book had it not been for help of many people, some of which have really gone out of their way to assist me with photographs and information. Firstly to Russell Coburn for tracking me down back in July 1998 via the Fantastic O's e-mail group, to ask 'Where is Neil K? We want another book'. This was a factor in persuading me to continue my writings on the O's after a break of over seven years.

Being the only Football League club historian based outside the UK, research has proved just a little more difficult then might be expected; without the help of the following people this book would not have been possible. I would firstly like to give special thanks to my brother Alan Kaufman, Alan J. Harvey and Martin P. Smith for regularly sending material to me in South Africa and to Beryl and Heini Wohl for bringing material over to me on their two trips to Africa.

A big 'Thank you' must go to the 300 or so members of Fantastic O's e-mail group, who have been a constant help and support to me over the past two years and to Paul West, for his financial support in purchasing old photographs. Thanks are also due to football historians Terry Frost, James Creasy, Gordon Macey and Andy Porter, as well as O's fans Ken Mortimer, Matthew Porter, Matthew Roper, Alan Ravenhill, Martin Strong, Mark S. Waters and Mark Wilson for their most wonderful help and ongoing assistance – always way beyond the call of duty.

Club photographer Tim Reder, Mike Childs, George Flower, Linda Mabbott (aka Species 8472), Tony Furby, Mark Priddy, Dave Read, Graham Smith, Chris Unwins, Alex White, Dave Winter (all the way from France), Jonathan Wren, *The Hackney Gazette*, *Ilford Recorder* and the *Walthamstow Guardian* are all owed a debt of gratitude for allowing me to reproduce their pictures.

Today's club owes its origins to former members of Homerton College, a theological teacher training college for non-Conformists and Puritans. In 1881 they formed themselves into the Glyn Cricket Club, matches being played in Victoria Park. The college was situated on the north side of 75 Homerton High Street. Over the next few years the club became a rather successful cricketing outfit. In 1886 the club changed its name to Eagle CC and in 1992 the college moved to Cambridge.

The following have also given generously of their valuable time:
Gbenga Aina, Johan Allard, Donald Allen, Peter Allen, Stu M. Allen, Herb Alpert, Association of Football Statisticians (AFS), Sean Baggaley, Erling Baldorf, Robert Barltrop, Peter Barnes, Graham Bell, David Bloomfield, Brian Blower, British Library Colindale, Keith Brookman, Andy Brown, Eddie Brown, Will Bryant of BBC Manchester, Trevor Bugg, Andrew Buonocore, James Burns, Denis Campbell, Richard Candler, Tim Carder, Scott Cheshire, Terry Cocklin, College of Arms, London, Alan Comfort, Bob Common, Tony Cowell, Bryan Daniels, Edwin's Music shop (New York, USA), Tron E. Enger, Sue & Kenny Etberg Design Studios, Jamie Evangelista, Jason Forrester, Ian Fuggle, Philip Geddes, Philip Glover, Richard Godwin, Graham Goodall, Malcolm Graham, Frank Grande, Terry Griffiths, Hackney Archives Department, Charlie Hasler, Brian Hill, John Hill, Derek Hitchcock, Keith Howard, David Hyams, Neil Johnston, Tommy Johnston, Jonathan Kaye, John Leech, Barney Lewis, Eddie Lewis, John Maddocks, Nick Madden, Ray Martin, Wade Martin, Rob Mellor, Johnny Meynell, Louise Michaelson, Len Mitty, Paul Morant, Paul Mullen, Donald Nannstad, Tom Nichol, the Nigerian FA, Matt Nolan, Fred Ollier, Ian Ochiltree, Orientear Fanzine, Michael R. Ovenden, Richard J. Owen, Ian Page, Max Page, Graham Paine, Adam Payne, Ralph Pokar, Dorothy Poss, Mike Peterson, P&O Shipping Group, James Pope, Mark Priddy, David Prowse, Mike Randall, Chris Richardson, Chris Roberts, Michael Robinson, David Russell, David Scally, Ian Sheen, Keith Simpson, Ray Simpson, Oliver Skelton, Mike Slater, Katy Snape, John Staff, Paul Staines, Martin Strong, Nicola Struthers, Ian Thomas, Brian and Phil Timms, David Tongue, Robert Trand, John Treleven, Roger J. Triggs, Dave Twydell, Leo Tyrie, Niam Uka, Gilbert Upton, Vestry House Museum in Walthamstow, Bob Walker, Waltham Forest Administration, Neil Watson, Julian Lloyd Webber, Roger Wedge, Judith West, Alex White, Windsor Castle Library, Brian B. Winston, Carl Yearwood, Chris Zoricich, Delia Zussman.

Finally, last but certainly not least, special thanks must go to my wife, Debbie, my twin daughters, Amy and Samantha, and the rest of my family for their constant prayers, support and understanding. Also to Stephen Etberg, Ferdy Kruger, Clive Franks, Merle Sandler and Paul Sandler, who have assisted me during my many computer crises.

Neilson N. Kaufman
South Africa, January 2001

One
Before the Great War

Part of the 24,600 crowd at Millfields Road for the visit of Manchester City on 6 March 1926 in a FA Cup quarter-final tie. Orient lost the encounter 1-6.

On the 3 March 1888, a meeting was held at 36 Dunlace Road, Lower Clapton, the home of club secretary R.P. 'Pomp' Haines, where two resolutions were passed that would give life to today's Leyton Orient Football Club. Club member Jack R. Dearing, a worker at the Orient Steamship Navigation Company (later taken over by the P&O Group) at the time of the launch of their first ship, the SS *Orient*, suggested that a football section be started and that it the name 'Orient' be adopted.

The 5,386-ton SS *Orient* steamship, was designed for the Australian mail service and built in Glasgow during 1879. It was used during the Boer war in South Africa in 1899 and returned to the Australian run in 1902. In 1909 it was sold to Italian ship-breakers.

Top, opposite page: After some uneventful seasons, 1893 saw the club join the Clapton & District League. Their colours were red shirts with a large, white, upper-case 'O' on their backs – thus the club's nickname came into being. To coincide with entry into the larger London League in 1898, the club changed its name to Clapton Orient FC. The O's amateur period culminated in 1902, with the winning of two cups: the West Ham Charity Cup (having defeated Clapton FC 1-0 in the final) and the Middlesex County Charity Cup (Ealing 1-0). In November 1903 the club turned professional. This team group is from 1902/03 and features the two trophies from the previous season. From left to right, back row: Mr A. Watson, Mr Osborne, Mr C. Howitt, Mr H.G. 'Tich' Woods (treasurer), Mr C.J. Lovelock (president), Mr E.A. 'Teddy' Wiggins (secretary and later the first club chairman), Mr E.H. Roberts, Mr J.T. Robinson. Third row: Mr J. Westrop, Mr A. Thompson, Mr A.E. Simpson, Alf Wallis (trainer/coach), Billy Price, Ernie Ward (goalkeeper), Bob Chalkley, Mr A. Unwin, Mr C. Jarvis, Mr Arthur Haines, Mr Symons (groundsman, standing behind Haines). Second row: Claude Berry, Ernie Bailey, Hugh McLelland. Front row: Ken Gibson, R.P. 'Pomp' Haines, Ginger Merritt, Jack Hills (captain), Bob McGeorge.

Below: In 1904, Orient entered a more serious stage in their history when they were elected into the Second Division of the Southern League. They finished seventh in their inaugural season, having gained 7 wins and a total of 21 points. Two of the players pictured in this 1904/05 team group – with their new strip of white shirts with red and green stripes and black shorts – are goalkeeper Joseph Redding (back row) and Herbert Charles Kingaby (the first player in the second row). Redding made 7 starts in Orient's first League campaign (1905/06), and let in 21 goals from 5 matches; he was so upset by this that he decided to retire. Hackney-born Kingaby was O's tricky wingman who, during the following season, recorded the club's first goal in the Football League. After 26 League matches for the O's, Bert joined Aston Villa in 1906 for a record fee of £300. Thereafter, he took Villa to court over the right of a transfer in a case that last many years – which, incidentally, he lost.

O 's reached their goal when they were elected to the Second Division of the Football League in May 1905, garnering 26 votes from the existing member clubs. Samuel Ormerod was appointed the club's first manager, having accumulated a lot of experience as secretary/manager with both Manchester City and Stockport County. Orient's big name signing was winger Richard Bourne from Preston North End, a tribunal fixing his fee at £100 in June 1905. The England trialist had made 62 appearances at Deepdale and had won a Second Division championship medal in 1904. The squad for the 1905/06 season was, from left to right, back row: Evenson, Wootten, Kingaby, Edward Alfred Wiggins (chairman), Charles James Lovelock (director), Codling, Bourne, G. Lamberton. Middle row: Boden, Dougal, Wilson (trainer), Horatio Bottomley (president), Ormerod (manager), J. Lamberton, McGeorge. Front row: Holmes, Boyle, James Thomas Robertson (director), Butler, Arthur Harvey Haines (director), Leigh, Proudfoot.

William Holmes, or 'Doc' as he was affectionately known, was born at Darley Hill Side, Matlock in 1875. He joined the O's from Manchester City on 19 August 1905 for £10, having played 156 League matches for the Hyde Road club. Holmes played a major part in Orient's early League history: after Ormerod resigned through ill health, Holmes was appointed player-manager in March 1906, making 51 senior appearances. He took over as full-time manager in March 1908, holding that position until his untimely death, when he collapsed in Hackney on 22 February 1922. His managerial acumen earned his side the title of 'Holmes' Homerton Heroes'. Holmes' managerial record was as follows: played 452, won 169, drew 100, lost 183; 515 goals were scored and 583 conceded.

The 1906/07 season was very important to Orient. Had they finished bottom of Division Two, they would have certainly lost their League status. Happily, seventeenth spot was attained. It was the performances of one player, William Martin (sitting at the end of the third row), with 17 goals that kept the team afloat. Twenty-three-year-old, Millwall-born Martin came from Hull City as a defender. He was converted to a forward and was Orient's top scorer for two seasons, scoring 30 senior goals from 64 games. Stockport County splashed out £150 for his services in May 1908.

During January 1906, Orient found themselves bottom of Division Two and in dire financial straits. The club was voluntarily wound up and an emergency committee was formed. The man to lead the fight was Henry Wells-Holland. Born in London on 8 June 1864, Wells-Holland had been Mayor of Hackney and a Bank of England official before joining the O's. He did a sterling job over the years in keeping the club in the Football League.

Left: Born in Manchester in 1882, Isaac Evenson was Orient's first League captain. He had joined the O's from Leicester Fosse in May 1905. This all-purpose footballer was the first O's player to score a League hat-trick, against Chesterfield in September 1905. Evenson also had a spell as manager, when Holmes was under suspension. Evenson was a fine servant during his two seasons with the club, moving on to West Bromwich Albion for £225 on 29 April 1907. *Right:* Sunderland-born John Thompson Johnston formed a formidable duo with George Johnson for five seasons. Johnston joined Orient from Middlesborough reserves in 1908, and missed just 10 matches in four seasons. Many sports writers suggested he should be capped for England, but his chance never came. He had to be content with 2 appearances for a Football League representative side against the Southern League. Johnston was awarded a benefit match in 1914.

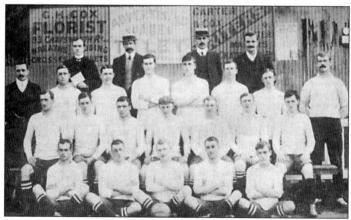

Clapton Orient, 1907/08. From left to right, back row: Mr Robinson (director), Mr Arber (director), Captain Henry Wells-Holland (chairman), Mr Goodger (director). Third row: William Holmes (manager), Reason, Henderson, Bower, W. Whittaker, Stewart, Bell, Wilson (trainer). Second row: Liddell, Shelley, Gates, Buchanan (wearing cap), Thacker, Howshall, Greechan. Front row: Parker, Leigh, Martin, Oliver, Pemberton. The O's improved to fourteenth position at the conclusion of this season. One of the more recent signings in the photograph is the man in the middle of the group wearing a cap – easily mistaken for the goalkeeper. He was thirty-three-year-old, Scottish-born right-half David Buchanan, who joined in 1906 from Southern League Plymouth Argyle. 'Buck' played with a black skull-cap to hide his baldness. Buchanan was a fine footballer, making 70 senior appearances before his appointment as player-manager of Southern League Leyton FC in 1908.

Over 20,000 spectators attended O's final League match, a 2-0 win over Leicester Fosse on 24 April 1915, before the players and officials left for war. This picture captures Orient skipper Fred Parker tossing the coin with visiting captain Horace Burton. Parker was one of the great characters in O's history and he played for eleven seasons, amassing 336 League appearances that yielded 34 goals.

Arthur Layton scores O's second goal in the final pre-First World War game against Leicester Fosse. This was only his third senior appearance that season, having netted 26 goals in the reserves. Twenty-five-year-old Layton played on during the war years, scoring 30 goals. He also made 23 League appearances in 1919/20, with 3 goals, before moving on to Northfleet in 1920.

Around forty Orient players and officials joined the Footballers' Battalion of the 17th Middlesex Regiment – this was the highest number from any football club. The players and officials are pictured here parading around the Millfields Road ground saying farewell to the fans on 24 April 1915. O's stars William Jonas and Richard McFadden are in the nearside column.

Left: A brilliant player, Richard McFadden is one of only a handful of truly prolific Orient goalscorers. Born in Cambuslang (Scotland) in 1890, he grew up in Blyth and joined Orient from Wallsend Park Villa in 1911. McFadden netted 19 goals in 1911/12 and 21 in 1914/15. He also starred in the England trial during November 1914. His 68 goals came from 142 senior appearances. *Right:* William Jonas was born Blyth in 1891. A friend of McFadden's, he joined the O's from Havanna Rovers – where he had scored 68 goals in two seasons – in 1912. Jonas proved an excellent capture with his fearless dashing style of play. He came to the fore in 1913/14, scoring 10 League goals and 17 reserve goals. Both he and McFadden were killed during the First World War, along with a third player, George Scott..

Two

Between the Wars

For the first season after the war, 1919/20, manager Holmes made some astute signings, including the three Tonner brothers. The Scottish Tonner brothers – from left to right, John, Samuel and James – made a unique record in football history during that season, appearing together in 12 League matches and an FA Cup tie. As far as Football League historians are aware, there have only been six sets of three brothers who played first team football together, the most recent being Danny, Ray and Rodney Wallace with Southampton in 1988/89. Unlike his two brothers, winger Jimmy could never break into the first team as a regular. Born in Bridgetown on 31 March 1896, he joined Orient from Dunfermline Athletic. James stayed just one season, before moving on to Scottish side Lochgelly United in 1920 and then Bo'ness. He returned to the League with Burnley in October 1924. John Tonner was the youngest of the brothers. An inside forward, John (also known as Jack) was born in Holytown on 20 February 1898. He also came to Orient from Dunfermline Athletic and eventually moved on to Fulham in 1926, having made 154 appearances and scored 39 goals. Following a two-year spell with the Cottagers, he moved to Crystal Palace before returning to Orient as a groundsman. In total, John made a total of 208 League appearances and scored 62 goals during his League career. He died in Southend in 1978. The eldest Tonner, Sam, was born Dunfermline on 10 August 1894. Like his brothers, he was also on the books of Dunfermline between 1912 and 1918, although he came to Orient via East Fife in July 1919. The right-back had remarkable speed and during the war years was the Army quarter-mile champion for four consecutive years. Sam Tonner made 194 appearances and scored 13 goals for Orient before joining Bristol City in July 1925. He died in Fleetwood in 1976.

Left: Born in Percy Main, Newcastle, outstanding twenty-two-year-old right half Billy Hind joined Orient from Fulham in May 1907 and stayed for seven seasons, playing 204 League and cup matches before hanging up his boots in 1920 to become trainer of Welsh club Ton Pentre. He returned to the O's as assistant trainer between December 1920 and 1925. *Right:* Tommy Dixon is yet another player to come from the north-east of England. Born in Seaham Harbour on 17 September 1899, he joined Orient in June 1919, after being spotted while playing for Murton Colliery Welfare. Dixon featured in the O's side for eight seasons, playing 244 matches and scoring 15 goals, before moving to Southend in 1927, where he made a further 265 senior appearances.

Clapton Orient Football Club, 1920/21. From left to right, back row: William Holmes (manager), Mr D. McCarthy (director), Mr A. Unwin (director), Mr H. Gray-Robbins (chairman), Mr R. Clarke (director), Hugall, Guy P. Dale, Mr E.F. Wimms (director), Mr C.W.H. Dean (secretary). Third row: Bradbury, Parker, S. Tonner, Forrest, Townrow, Nicholson, Nicholls, Osmond. Second row: Leggett, Hasney, Cockle, Smith, Gillatt, Juniper, J. Tonner, Williams, Dixon, Fred Powell (trainer). Front row: Nunn, Warboys. The O's, still in Division Two, improved to seventh place during this season. However, a tragedy had occurred on 14 December 1920 when Guy P. Dale was killed in a motor accident in Faringham, Kent. A very promising goalkeeper, he had recently joined the club from Barnsley and played just one League match for Orient – a 1-0 win at Bury in October.

Skipper James Hugall presents the Orient players to the Prince of Wales on a Royal visit during 1921.

Cover of the souvenir programme that commemorated the visit of The Prince of Wales to Millfields Road on 30 April 1921 for the Division Two League match versus Notts County. O's won the game 3-0.

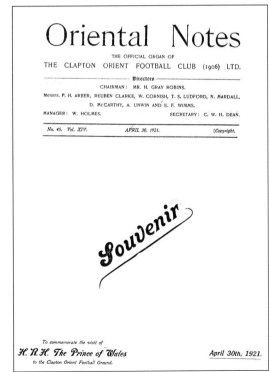

His Royal Highness the Duke of York (later to be crowned King George VI), sitting with the Orient directors, April 1922. From left to right, back row: Mr A. Unwin, Mr E.F. Wimms, -?-, Mr C.W.J. Cornish, -?-, Mr D. McCarthy, Mr T.S. Ludford, Mr N. Mardall. Front row: Mr P.H. Arber, HRH The Duke of York, Mr H. Gray-Robbins (chairman).

The cover of the souvenir programme that commemorated the visit of The Duke of York to Millfields Road on 22 April 1922 for the Division Two League match against Bristol City, which Orient lost 0-1.

Owen Williams became the first Orient player to gain full international honours when he played for England against Ireland at West Bromwich on 22 October 1922. He made both goals in a 2-0 win. Williams gained one further cap, against Wales, in 1923. This small stocky winger, born in Ryhope, County Durham on 23 September 1895 was arguably the finest left-winger in the O's history. After 170 matches and 25 goals he was transferred to First Division Middlesbrough in March 1924 for £2,525. Williams played in the North-East for seven seasons before, having played in 194 senior matches and scored 43 goals, joining Southend United in August 1930 for £300. Williams died in Easington on 9 December 1960.

Clapton Orient FC, 1921/22. Having joined the club in 1910, this was to be James Cockburn Hugall's final season after the arrival of Arthur Wood. Having enjoyed eight wonderful seasons with Orient, the Sunderland-born custodian joined Durham FC in 1922. He died on 23 September 1927, aged just thirty-nine. From left to right, back row: Mr C.W.H. Dean (secretary), Mr N. Mardell (director), Mr A. Unwin (director), Mr E.F. Wimms (director), Wood, S. Gough, Hugall, Mr D. McCarthy (director), Mr T.S. Ludford (director), Mr P.H. Arber (director), Mr H. Gray-Robbins (chairman). Third row: Mr W. Holmes (manager), F. Powell (trainer), Bradbury, Dixon, Townrow, Whipp, Cheriton, Forrest, Nicholson, Nicholls, Worboys, Osmond, W. Hind (assistant trainer), F. Bevan (reserve coach). Second row: Smith, Leggett, E. Williams, Gillatt, Parker, Rennox, Bratby, Denton, O. Williams. Front row: S. Tonner, Kean, Nunn, J. Tonner. Clatworthy 'Charlie' Rennox was born in Shotts, Scotland in 1897. A powerful centre forward, he joined Orient from Wisham FC and was eventually transferred to Manchester United in March 1925 for £1,250.

The story of Albert Arthur Pape makes remarkable reading. The bustling centre forward made just 24 League appearances for O's, scoring 11 goals, yet he still had time to write his name in Orient history by virtue of his bizarre transfer to Manchester United on 7 February 1925. Whilst sitting with the other O's players in the Old Trafford visitors' dressing room, the papers from the Football League necessary to ratify his £2,000 transfer were received, via wire, by O's chairman Gray-Robbins and his United counterpart George H. Lawton. The crowd of 18,250 were stunned at the news, as Pape quickly changed dressing rooms and put on a United shirt, before going on to score United's third goal in a 4-2 victory. A man of many clubs, Pape scored 103 League goals from 266 appearances in the course of his career.

A great O's player, John Ernest Townrow was the second player to gain full international recognition whilst with Orient. A centre-half noted for his power, coolness, heading ability and accurate passing, he was first spotted by manager Proudfoot playing for England Schoolboys versus Scotland and Wales in 1915. He was signed as a professional after the war in July 1919. He won his first full England cap against Scotland at Hampden Park in 1925. One further cap followed against Wales in 1926. After eight seasons, 265 senior appearances and 5 goals, he moved on, for a record transfer fee of over £3,000, to Chelsea in February 1927. Townrow had three successful years at Stamford Bridge, making 130 League appearances. He died in Knarsborough on 11 April 1969.

Left: action from Orient's game against Bury at Millfields Road on 29 September 1923. The O's won the encounter 1-0. Thirty-year-old, Liverpool-born Thomas Green, playing in only his seventh game for the club, is seen here challenging the Bury 'keeper, Richardson. Having joined Orient from Stockport County in May 1923, Green ended the season as Orient's top League goalscorer with 10 in 24 appearances. He moved to Hearts in February 1924. *Right:* A week later at Millfields, Orient lost 0-1 to Leeds. In this photograph, forward Herbert Bliss is putting in a defensive header as centre-half Townrow provides cover.

Having finished tenth in Division Two at the end of the 1923/24 season, Orient went on tour to Denmark. This team group, pictured in Copenhagen in May 1924, is made up of, from left to right, back row: Mr C.W.H. Dean (secretary), -?-, Mr D. McCarthy (director), Mr E.P. Wimms (director), Mr T.S. Ludford (director), Gailbraith, Townrow, Smith, Nicholson, Wood, Rosier, Powell (trainer), -?-, -?-, Mr C.W.J. Cornish (director), -?-, Peter Proudfoot (manager). Front row: Nunn, Dixon, Sam Tonner, Hannaford, Jack Tonner, -?-, -?-, -?-.

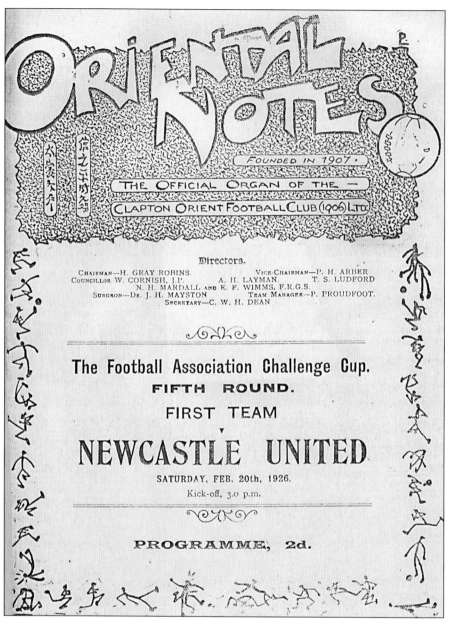

ORIENTAL NOTES

· FOUNDED IN 1907 ·

THE OFFICIAL ORGAN OF THE —

CLAPTON ORIENT FOOTBALL CLUB (1906) LTD.

Directors.

CHAIRMAN—H. GRAY ROBINS.   VICE-CHAIRMAN—P. H. ARBER
COUNCILLOR W. CORNISH, J.P.   A. H. LAYMAN.   T. S. LUDFORD
N. H. MARDALL AND E. F. WIMMS, F.R.G.S.
SURGEON—DR. J. H. MAYSTON   TEAM MANAGER—P. PROUDFOOT.
SECRETARY—C. W. H. DEAN

The Football Association Challenge Cup.

FIFTH ROUND.

FIRST TEAM

v

NEWCASTLE UNITED

SATURDAY, FEB. 20th, 1926.

Kick-off, 3.0 p.m.

PROGRAMME, 2d.

On 20 February 1926, Orient faced the mighty Newcastle United in the FA Cup fifth round. The match attracted an attendance of 31,400, who paid receipts of over £2,600. The unexpected happened on 23 minutes: Peter Gavigan took a corner, a melee occurred, and the ball came to John Gailbraith – who hit a stunning shot from 25 yards all along the ground and into the net. Donald Cock scored a second goal for Orient on 45 minutes and O's defence held out in the second half to clinch the tie. As the final whistle went the fans swarmed onto the pitch to chair their heroes from the field. A number of jubilant fans carried off the sixteen-stone Arthur Wood, who was smiling all the way to the tunnel. This game still ranks as one of the club's all-time greatest victories and was the very first time that the O's had defeated a team from the top flight of the Football League; the Magpies were lying sixth in Division One at the time. Over 35,000 of these programmes were sold that day.

Top: Skipper Arthur Wood leads the Orient players out onto the pitch for fifth round FA Cup tie against Newcastle. Remarkably, this was his 202nd consecutive senior appearance. *Middle:* Dixon heads clear from Gallacher whilst Orient defenders Evans, Townrow and Broadbent look on. *Bottom:* Goalkeeper Wood challenges the legendary Scottish international centre forward Hughie Gallacher.

Clapton Orient FC team group, 1926/27. From left to right, back row: F. Powell (trainer), A. King, J. Rutherford, A. Wood, A. Slater, A. Campbell, W. Carey, W. Hind (assistant trainer). Third row: P. Proudfoot (manager), A. Lyons, F. McCudden, J.Gailbraith, T. Evans, J. Townrow, W. Hayward, H. Spence, W. Broadbent, H. Ashton, J. Dixon, Mr C. Dean (secretary). Second row: B. Rosier, R. Dennison, Mr B. Emanuel (director), Mr C.W.J. Cornish (director), Mr G. Harris (director), S. Baxter, G. Streets. Front row: (inset) W. Nesbitt, J. Gardner, J. Mooney, D. Cock, J. Yardley, W. Corkindale. This worn picture is not included because of the mascot dog, but because it contains a couple of unique players. Firstly, the balding player in the top row is John Rutherford. Known as Jack, he was a legend in his own time. Born in Percy Main, Newcastle-upon-Tyne on 12 October 1884, Rutherford made 513 senior appearances for both Newcastle United and Arsenal, scoring 100 goals. During this time he played in five FA Cup finals and an FA Cup final replay. Rutherford joined Orient on 17 August 1926 and made 9 appearances. His final game was a 4-5 home defeat by Portsmouth in April 1927. Aged 42 years and 172 days, he became the oldest player to appear for O's in a League match – until some thirty-nine years later when forty-seven-year-old Peter Shilton arrived in 1996. Rutherford died in Neasden on 21 April 1963. The other remarkable character in the photograph is the player third from the right in the third row, Hubert Ashton. Born in Calcutta on 13 February 1898, Ashton will be not remembered for his 6 League appearances – 5 of them with Orient and the other with Bristol Rovers – as an amateur player, or for his cricketing career with both Cambridge and Essex CCC. It is for his political career that he will go down in history, having spent fourteen years as Conservative MP for Chelmsford (1950-1964), four years as personal private secretary to the Chancellor of the Exchequer and then the Home Secretary in 1957. Ashton was created a Knight of the British Empire in 1956. Sir Hubert was later chairman of Essex CCC (1941-1950) and then president (1955-1969). He was also president of the MCC during the controversial South African cricket crisis of 1960-61. Hubert Ashton died in South Weald, Essex in June 1979.

Born in Maerdy, Wales on 7 April 1903, Tom Evans was a tall, athletic and skilful full-back, who joined Orient from Maerdy FC in May 1924. Injured after one appearance at Southampton in September 1924, he moved on loan to Aberdare Town, making 5 League appearance for the Welsh club, before rejoining the O's in December 1925. Evans became Orient's third player to gain international honours when he played for Wales against Scotland at Ibrox on 30 October 1926. He gained 2 further caps while with the O's before transferring to Newcastle United in December 1927 for £3,650. Plagued with knee injuries throughout his time in the North-East, he returned to Orient in 1930, before moving to Merthyr Town in 1932. Evans played a total of 87 senior matches for Orient and scored 1 goal.

Clapton Orient, 1927/28. From left to right, back row: Mr B. Emanuel (director), Peter Proudfoot (manager), Sage, Campbell, Slater, Wood, Lyons, Whipp, Fred Powell (trainer). Third row: Mr C.W.H. Dean (secretary), Gailbraith, Duffy, Smith, Surtees, Hope, Evans, Spence, Armstrong, Broadbent, Corkindale. Second row: Jewhurst, Williams, Mr G. Harris (director), Mr P.H. Arber (vice chairman), Mr T.S. Ludford (chairman), Councillor C.W.J. Cornish (director), Streets, Dennison. Front row: Collins, Gardner, Kerr. Orient just escaped relegation at the end of this campaign, at the expense of Fulham. The Craven Cottage club's management complained to the Football League that the O's manager, Peter Proudfoot, had pre-arranged certain match results. The FA inquiry reported that the allegations were unfounded. Despite clearing him of the original charges, however, they found that he had acted irregularly in other matters and suspended him for six months. Proudfoot resigned, yet stayed with the club in various office and managerial positions until January 1939. He still holds the record for being the manager in charge for the highest number of League matches. During Proudfoot's time as manager, Orient played 483, won 148, drew 117 and lost 218 games, scoring 566 goals and conceding 742.

At Villa Park

Aston Villa 0, Clapton Orient 0.

The visit of Clapton Orient to Villa Park in the Fourth Round of the Cup will be remembered by Aston Villa for many a day, and it may be questioned whether a more disappointing game has been played on the classic sward—from the Villa point of view, of course. The view of the Orient and their supporters, who were present in force, was of a distinctly different tint, and they were naturally cock-a-hoop when the whistle sounded, and we had failed to claim the right to go forward. It must be said that our opponents played their own game with conspicuous determination, and that with only ten men throughout the second half, they were heavily handicapped.

There was a fine assembly to see this match, 53,000 spectators being present, and there was all the usual Cup-tie excitement. After our splendid show against West Ham, it was thought that a repetition would take us sailing away to the Fifth Round. That was a justifiable notion. Instead, we played a game as unconvincing as any game could be. The conditions were bad, 'tis true; but no worse for us than for our opponents, who appeared less affected by the difficulties, and forced our players to play the game they wanted.

As had been expected, there was one change in our team—at left half-back—Tate not having recovered from his shoulder injury, and Swales, who has shown excellent promise in Reserve games, was called up to deputise. He did excellently, and made a very good impression by his capable footwork, careful feeding, and dour determination. But, generally, it was our "off" day. Mention must be made of an offside goal scored by our opponents, when the game was 37 minutes old. Though the Clapton players appealed vigorously for this to be allowed, the referee was firm in his refusal—as he was morally bound to be, seeing that he whistled before the ball was actually netted. Altogether, a sad show—from the Villa point of view, and so we will no longer contemplate it.

ASTON VILLA: Olney; Smart, Bowen; Kingdon, Talbot, Swales; York, Beresford, Waring, Walker, Chester.

CLAPTON ORIENT: Wood; Morley, Gay; Galbraith, Eastman, Duffy; Collins, Whipp, Turnbull, Dennison, Corkindale.

At Homerton.

Clapton Orient 0, Aston Villa 8.

There was a truer Villa ring about the replay in which we engaged at Homerton on Wednesday. The conditions had changed for the better, and instead of a frozen ground we had the felicity of performing on a space that allowed a player to exhibit his skill. The result was that after our opponents had, in an ecstacy of hope, set out to force our lines, they found the attacked playing the part of attackers so ably and well, that the hope that had buoyed them up was dissipated after about ten minutes. Thereafter Clapton Orient had no chance of winning. Villa players pulled together in such purposeful fashion as to deny the opposition any serious say as to the disposition of the honours.

Only two goals came before the interval, but afterwards they came in spate, and the final total might well have been more than eight, which, by the way, were shared by six players—all the forwards and Swales. If there were goals more finely obtained than others, they were those by Swales, Beresford and Dorrell. The former's was despatched from well outside the penalty area, the ball coming in from Dorrell after rounding Morley; Beresford's was the first after the interval, a spectacular effort with a ball that had not yet come to earth—a surpriser; Dorrell's was the sort of shot an outside forward should specialise in—a catapult shot while in full flight, for they do so tease a goalkeeper.

Waring's three, and he narrowly missed making it four, will make him greedy for more; Dick York's was a topper, and came after a very tricky pass by Beresford; and Cook's was a walk-in.

The Orient deserve congratulation for playing to the finish with adamantine pluck, realising as they must have done the hopelessness of their task. That must have been plain to them, for the speed, resource and execution of the Villa players was on a plane altogether too high. Their right back, Morley, was a tower of strength to his side, and he stood out from all his fellows.

CLAPTON ORIENT: Wood; Morley, Gay; Galbraith, Eastman, Duffy; Collins, Whipp, Turnbull, Dennison, Corkindale.

ASTON VILLA: Olney; Smart, Bowen; Kingdon, Talbot, Swales; York, Beresford, Waring, Cook, Dorrell.

After an excellent but unexpected display to knock Southampton out of the FA Cup, Orient were drawn to play away against high-riding First Division Aston Villa. With O's having lost 13 League matches during the season, they were given little chance of avoiding a heavy defeat. The match at Villa Park, played on a frozen pitch, was witnessed by 53,086 – the largest attendance ever to watch an O's match. Orient bravely held out for a goal-less draw. The replay at Homerton, played on the following Wednesday afternoon, attracted 27,532 spectators, who witnessed the O's being demolished 8-0 in their highest ever first-class defeat. This illustration is the view of the two matches from Aston Villa's programme, *Villa Record and News*, of 2 February 1929.

The cartoon depicts Orient's 3-1 home win over Coventry City and Reg Tricker's winning goal at Walsall. Unfortunately, as requested by the cartoonist, the London teams did not oblige. The O's lost 2-4 at home to QPR but drew 2-2 at Fulham, the match at Craven Cottage attracting a crowd of 17,012. The Orient players in the cartoon are referred to as 'Chinks', in reference to the O's Chinaman mascot. Orient played their final match at Millfields Road during May of this season. Their League record at the ground, from 9 September 1905 to 3 May 1930, was as follows: played 421, won 219, drew 108, lost 94; goals for 633, goals against 362.

In 1930, Orient had to leave their Millfields Road ground after thirty years because of pressure from the greyhound racing syndicate. The club moved to Lea Bridge Road, just half a mile away. In November 1930, after Torquay United were beaten 4-0, they complained to FA that the wooden fencing around the stadium was too close to the pitch. In the meantime, permission was granted by the FA to play two home League matches at the famous Wembley Stadium. In their first game at the national ground, the O's defeated Brentford 3-0 in front of 8,319 fans. The second match, two weeks later, saw them defeat Southend United 3-1.

The match on 18 April 1931, a 3-2 victory against Luton Town, marked the end of an era, as it was the final home game for Orient's legendary goalkeeper Arthur Wood – who received a thunderous ovation from the 5,078 crowd. Wood totalled 395 senior matches, the record for the most appearances for the club until it was broken by Peter Allen in 1976. Wood still holds the record for consecutive League matches played: 225 between 3 September 1921 and 4 December 1926. He moved to Ryde Sports on the Isle of Wight and later played for Newport (Isle of Wight). Arthur Wood died in Portsmouth on 8 April 1941 at the age of forty-seven. Here, Captain Jack Fowler is shaking hands with new manager Jimmy Seed.

The story of Tommy Mills is quite a remarkable one. Born in Ton Petre, Wales on 28 December 1911, he was capped as a Welsh schoolboy. However, it seemed that the chance of a League career had passed him by when he began working as a miner before moving to London to work in the Trocadero Hotel. He was spotted playing for the hotel staff team in the Sunday League and made his Orient debut at Brighton on 25 September 1929. He blossomed to become a brilliant creative player with splendid ball control. The first of his 2 Welsh caps gained while with the O's came against England in November 1933, when he scored the winning goal. After 132 senior appearances he moved to Leicester City for £2,000 in 1934. Mills died after being knocked down by a lorry in Bristol on 15 May 1979.

Left: Frederick John Sidney Le May was born in Bethnal Green on 2 February 1907. A right-winger, he joined Orient from Watford in 1932. He is reputed to be the smallest player ever to appear in the Football League – he was only 5ft tall. Despite his small stature, Le May starred in a 7-1 win over Swindon Town in January 1933. He made 10 League appearances for the O's before joining Margate in 1933. *Right:* David Hyman Morris, known as 'Abe', was one of many top-quality Jewish players to have played for Orient over the years, along with stars like Metchick, Lazarus and Silkman. Morris was one of the most prolific goalscorers of his era, notching up 290 from 420 outings over a thirteen-year career. He joined Orient as a thirty-six-year-old and managed 11 League and cup goals in just 15 matches before being replaced by newly-signed veteran David Halliday. Morris then scored 23 goals for the reserves before moving on to Cheltenham Town in 1934. He died in San Mateo, California in December 1985 at the age of eighty-eight.

New manager David Pratt, the former Celtic and Liverpool player, was like a breath of fresh air at Orient. This picture shows Pratt, first on the left in top row, with some of the twenty-six new players signed for the 1935/36 season. One of the newcomers was the brilliant Dunfries-born forward David Halliday. The thirty-six-year-old joined the O's from Arsenal for £1,500 after a wonderful career with Dundee and Sunderland. The 5ft 11ins striker had a trademark short shuffling stride which took him over the ground quickly. He scored 36 goals from just 55 senior appearances for Orient. In fifteen years of Scottish and English League football, he scored a total of 338 goals and averaged an amazing 0.751 goals per game. Also in this squad photograph is thirty-nine-year-old full-back Thomas Lucas, last in the middle row, who made 25 senior appearances in 1933/34, before leaving to become manager of Orient nursery club Ashford Town. Lucas had made 366 senior appearances for Liverpool between 1919 and 1933 and had won 3 England caps. From left to right, back row: David Pratt (manager), Austin, French, Halliday, Keen, Pickett, Robertson, Hillam, Farrell, Coull, Finlayson, Wright, Stan White (trainer). Middle row: McAninly, Ware, Taylor, Fogg, Fellowes, Rigby, Crawford, Manns, Lucas. Front row: Henderson, Mayson, Crompton, Miles, Millington, Stevens, Foster.

This team group was taken in January 1936 with Peter Proudfoot back as boss. The last player pictured in the third row is Edmund Crawford. Twenty-eight-year-old Ted Crawford came from Liverpool, yet made his name at Halifax Town with 21 goals from 30 League appearances in 1931/32. He joined Orient in July 1933 and demonstrated what powerful shooting was all about, breaking O's scoring record with 23 goals in the season. In total, Crawford scored 73 senior goals from 212 matches. From left to right, back row: E. Ware, V. Farrell, D. Affleck, G. Woods. Third row: S.E. White (trainer), W. Trodd, G. Heinemann, F. Searle, D. Wall, C. Hillam, G. Pateman, B. Herod, J. Taylor, W. Wright (assistant trainer). Second row: P. Proudfoot (manager), R. Quinn, G. Reed, H. Smith, A. Hurst, E. Edwards, J. Mayson, V. Hammond, E. Crawford, T.W. Halsey (secretary). Front row: L. Caiels, H. Campbell, W. Fogg, I. Miles, H. Taylor, T. Foster.

After seven seasons at Lea Bridge Road, O's moved to their new home at Brisbane Road, Leyton – known at the time as the Osborne Road Ground. The first League match at the ground took place on 28 August 1937. It was against Cardiff City and finished as a 1-1 draw. Fred Tully scored the Orient goal in front of 14,598 fans. This photograph shows the players being presented to the president of the Football League. From left to right: Codling, Taylor, Searle (the captain, who is shaking hands with Mr C.E. Sutcliffe, the president of the Football League), Hearty, Smith, Hillam, Lane, Bartlett, Fletcher and Tully.

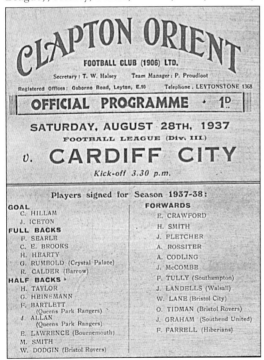

The cover of the programme for the first match at Brisbane Road.

This is the Orient squad for the 1939/40 season, which was eventually abandoned after just three League matches due to the outbreak of the Second World War. All records for those matches were expunged from the record books. From left to right, back row: W. Bunyon, R. Ranson, S. Hall, R. Williams, J. Ellis, J. McNeil. Middle row: W.P Wright (trainer), R. Black, H. Taylor, L. Allum, G. Rumbold, F. Bartlett, R. Bungay, F. Hanley, A. Young, S. Barnes, H. Smith, J. Pugsley (assistant trainer). Front row: W. McFadyen, Tully, R. Shankly, J. Harvey, L. Hann, Mr T.W. Halsey (secretary/manager), G. Willshaw, E. Crawford, T. Turner, A. Barraclough, L. Gore. One of the players in this photograph, Les Gore, later became coach and manager with Orient between 1950 and 1966. Thirty-five-year-old Scottish international William McFadyen had made his mark with Motherwell, scoring 53 goals from 38 appearances in 1931/32 with a total of 251 goals from 278 Scottish League appearances for the 'Wells between 1921 and 1936. Also in this team group is the first black player on Orient's books: Frederick Hanley had joined the O's from Chelsea reserves, but due to the outbreak of war never got his chance to make a senior debut.

Pictured before the start of the 1947/48 season are George Skelton, Wally Pullen and Victor Ralph Johnson. George Alfred Skelton was born in Thurcroft, near Rotherham, on 2 November 1919. He started his footballing career with Thurcroft Welfare FC, turning professional with Huddersfield Town in December 1945. He made just one League appearance with Huddersfield, losing 3-0 at Sunderland in September 1946. He became an 'Oriental' on 29 July 1947. After just 3 League appearances, his last a 6-0 defeat at Bristol City on 17 September 1947, he sustained a serious rib injury which forced him to retire from the game. Skelton died in Thurcroft in September 1994, just before his seventy-fifth birthday.

Captain Charles Hewitt (above) was appointed as manager on 1 January 1946. There were high expectations, as he had previously guided Chester from the Cheshire League up into the Football League. He had also taken Millwall to promotion and an FA Cup semi-final place. However, things did not work out for him at Orient. He often pleaded for funds for new players, but his requests fell on deaf ears and on 20 September 1946 he resigned and was replaced by the O's coach, and former Bolton Wanderers and Reading player, William Bulloch Wright (left). Wright had already enjoyed spells as coach with French club Rouen and Crystal Palace in 1939. He spent six years in the forces, before joining Orient as the team coach in 1946. He was manager for less than two weeks and took the club through just 2 League matches – the shortest reign of any O's manager – as Hewitt was invited back to the club as secretary-manager on 9 October 1946. In 1948 Wright joined his namesake, and former O's manager during the war years, William P. Wright as coach of Chingford Town. Hewitt was fired in April 1948.

Three

Promotion and Tommy Johnston

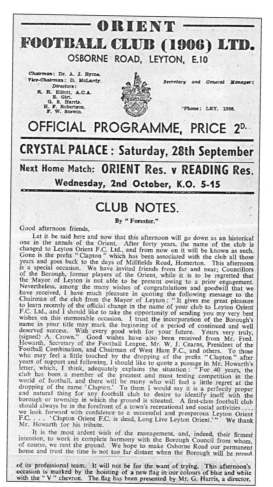

After forty years the name of the club was changed to Leyton Orient – nine years after they actually moved to the Borough of Leyton. The programme editor was not quite correct in his article, the title 'Clapton Orient' was first introduced in June 1898, forty-eight years previously.

Unlike current Premiership players, professionals after the Second World War were not in the super-tax bracket, earning just £4 per week. Twenty-seven-year-old centre half Ronald Duncan Sales joined Orient from Newcastle United, having playing 42 wartime games for the Magpies, in 1947. After making 28 senior appearances, he joined Hartlepool United in August 1950. Ronnie Sales retired in 1952 because of a knee injury. With no nest egg to fall back on, he had to work as a fitter for Reyrolles's. Sales spent his final year in hospital with Alzheimer's disease and died in August 1996. In this photograph, Ronnie Sales (right) is pictured with Billy Stroud and William 'Buster' Brown.

Left: Powerful twenty-six-year-old centre forward Frank Neary was Orient's top League goalscorer in the early seasons after the war. In 1948/49 he broke Edmund Crawford's record of 23 League goals with 25. In total, he netted 44 goals from 81 senior appearances for the O's. In October 1949, Neary joined QPR for £7,500. After just 10 appearances and 4 goals, he moved on to Millwall, where he scored 50 goals in 123 appearances. *Right:* Glasgow-born forward George Sutherland came to Brisbane Road from Partick Thistle, where he bagged 33 goals. He laid claim to one O's record – which is still unbroken to this day – by scoring a hat-trick twice against a particular club in one season. In November 1949 Sutherland scored three goals in the 4-4 draw at Ipswich Town; he achieved the same feat in the corresponding home fixture during January 1950, ending the season on 16 goals from 29 appearances.

William Derek Rees is handed his Welsh international cap – which he had obtained whilst with Spurs, for whom he only played 11 matches, for an encounter with Northern Ireland in the summer of 1950 – from O's chairman Harry Zussman before the game against Reading on 26 August 1950. Rees' home debut attracted a crowd of 21,298. Also in the picture, from left to right, are: Alex Stock (manager), Frank Harris (director), Monty Bell (club doctor) and Arthur Page (director). Rees had a wonderful career at Leyton, scoring 66 goals from 198 senior appearances. He died in Bridgend on 25 July 1996.

Seventeen-year-old Brian Jackson made his League debut on 30 December 1950 against Southend. After some wonderful displays down the right wing, one top soccer writer had even dared to suggest that Jackson was better than Stanley Matthews at the same age. After just 38 League appearances, Jackson joined Liverpool for £7,500 plus winger Donald Woan in November 1951: this was a substantial fee for a youngster in those days. He was no failure at Anfield, making 131 senior appearances and scoring 12 goals.

The Orient team in the dressing room before facing Arsenal at Leyton in an FA Cup fifth round tie on 23 February 1952. One player who burst into prominence was Feltham-born Dennis Pacey, who netted a hat-trick on his senior debut versus Gorleston in a second round reply at Highbury in December 1951. Pacey scored 12 FA Cup goals – more than any other O's player. From left to right, back row: Jimmy Richardson (assistant trainer), Les Blizzard, Stan Aldous, Pat Welton, Arthur Banner, Jackie Deverall, Les Gore (trainer). Front row: Des Woan, Dennis Pacey, Tommy Harris, Alec Stock (manager), Tommy Brown, Paddy Blatchford, John Evans.

At Orient's open day in 1954 are Welshman Stanley Morgan (left), an inside forward who joined from Millwall in 1953, and Canada-born forward Michael Burgess (right). Morgan started with Arsenal and played for O's in their First Division Championship-winning side of 1955/56, at the age of thirty-five. Burgess formed part of the deal that brought the legendary Tommy Johnston from Newport County two years later. He made a career total of 314/1 League appearance, scoring 58 goals for Orient.

At the end of the 1954/55 season, Orient finished second in Division Three (South), nine points behind champions Bristol City. One of the more satisfying results was a 4-1 win over City on 1 January 1955. Johnny Hartburn is pictured here scoring in front of 20,347 spectators in that match. Later, in the mid-1960s, Hartburn was appointed as the O's first-ever pools promoter, and died in January 2001.

The 1955/56 season was one for the record books, with Orient finishing as Division Three (South) champions. This was their first major success in the Football League and the only season in which over 100 League goals were scored by an O's team. The campaign was not without controversy; in November 1956, fans' favorites Vic Groves and Stan Charlton were sold to Arsenal for a joint fee of £30,000. Groves is pictured here at his home, just after his signing, with his many trophies and pictures. He stayed at Highbury for nine years, making 203 senior appearances and scoring 47 goals.

Ronald Heckman scored five goals in an FA Cup first round tie against Lovells Athletic on 19 November 1955. In doing so, he became the only O's player to achieve this number of goals in a senior match. Heckman is pictured here at his home with the match ball at the bottom of the shelf. He scored a total of 44 senior goals in 87 appearances during his three seasons with Orient. Ronnie died at Bracknell on 26 November 1990.

The man to take over from Alec Stock, who joined Arsenal, was Coventry-born Frederick Lesley Gore, affectionately known as 'Les'. In this 1956 photograph, Gore is being presented with a special pen, inscribed with his record of 10 wins and 1 defeat, by Stock, who returned after just 53 days.

Tommy Johnston scoring the winner on his debut at Swindon Town on 26 February 1956. The signing of O's legendary goalscorer Tommy Johnston was something of a joint effort between players and management. It was skipper Stan Aldous who initially suggested that Orient sign Johnston from Newport County. No one was more surprised than Aldous when he heard a month later that the Welsh club had accepted £4,000 and Mike Burgess in exchange for Johnston.

March 1956 was a wonderful period in Orient's history, with the team scoring 21 League goals in just 5 matches. Welshman Philip Woosnam is in action here, scoring in an 8-3 win over Aldershot. Woosnam won a Welsh international cap against Scotland in 1959, just before his £30,000 transfer to West Ham United. Later, he became a major influence on the growth of soccer in America.

41

Johnny Hartburn's corner kick finds its way into the net in a match against Millwall in 1956, edging Orient closer to the Division Three (South) championship. Aldous, Johnston and Woosnam are the players turning in celebration – this could have been a little premature as Summers equalised for the Lions at The Den on 30 April 1956.

THAT'S IT!

Orient are there

GLORY DAY! Leyton Orient's winning goal that sends them into the Second Division is shot in by centre-forward, Tom Johnston.

Tommy Johnston drives home the winner and the 22,377 crowd can celebrate the first title in the O's history. The 1955/56 season was a closely fought contest: Orient finished one point clear of second-placed Brighton (with an inferior goal difference) and two points clear of Ipswich Town, who were in third position.

Orient's 1955/56 Division Three (South) championship squad. This team photograph was taken straight after the Millwall match. From left to right, back row: Gore (trainer), Nichols, Heckman, Hartburn, McMahon, Facey, Webb, Gregory, Lee, Welton, Bishop, Julians, Johnston, Earl, Smith, Collins (assistant trainer). Front row: White, Blizzard, Aldous (captain), McKnight, Woosnam, Hartburn.

Stanley Aldous, O's skipper, with boss Alec Stock in the dressing room after the Millwall match. Born in Northfleet in 1923, Aldous captained Orient during some of their greatest triumphs and the powerful centre-half is one of a rare band to have made over 300 senior appearances for the club. When speaking to the author some years ago, he said 'Much of the credit for what was achieved that season had to go to the undoubting spirit of the supporters. How they boosted our morale, game after game.' Aldous died in Ely on 17 October 1995.

O's new main stand, purchased from the derelict Mitcham Stadium, being erected for the start of the 1956/57 season. The final south wing was not added until 1962.

Orient's first goal back in Division Two, after a break of twenty-seven years, being headed home by twenty-six-year-old Dave Sexton against Nottingham Forest on 18 August 1956 in front of 25,272 spectators. Sexton, after a brief spell as O's manager in 1965, later became a successful League manager and England's assistant manager under Bobby Robson in 1983.

The players celebrate Phil White's twenty-sixth birthday in the dressing room at Bury on 29 December 1956. Orient won the game 3-1. White (bottom centre), along with Willemse and Facey White, was arguably one of the best ever crossers of a football and much of Tommy Johnston's success was due to his perfectly weighted balls into the box. Phil White died in June 2000, aged seventy.

The largest attendance for the 1956/57 season came when 27,576 turned up for the visit of Chelsea in an FA Cup third round tie on 3 January. To celebrate the occasion, O's reverted to their old white shirts with a red chevron. Pictured before the match are Orient's three former Blues – Jimmy Smith, Stan Willemse and Phil McKnight. Orient lost the match 2-0.

Orient had some real characters in their squad for the 1959/60 season. At the back of this team group is Manchester-born Eddie Lewis. A former Busby babe, at sixty-five he is still involved in soccer for club and country in South Africa. In the third row are veterans Tommy Johnston, Eddie Baily and Eddie Brown. Clapton-born Baily had a long career with Spurs, appearing in 296 League matches and scoring 64 goals. He played just 29 matches for Orient. Baily was coach when Orient were promoted to Division One in 1962 and currently lives in retirement at Enfield. Brown, who lives in Fulwood, Preston, once said 'Look at me still coaching at seventy-four; I have one foot in the grave and the other on a banana skin'. He played over 400 matches with over 200 goals during his career. These three veterans, with a combined age of 112 years at the time, steered O's to tenth spot in Division Two, Johnston and Brown scoring 37 League goals between them. From left to right, back row: Cyril Lea, Ronnie Foster, Eddie Lewis, Peter Burridge, George Wright. Third row: Ken Facey, Sid Bishop, Frank George, Dave Groombridge, Stan Charlton, Nick Collins (trainer). Second row: George Waites, Tommy Johnston, Eddie Baily, Eddie Brown, Joe Elwood. Front row: Phil White, Malcolm Lucas. Sadly, three players pictured, Waites, White and Wright, all died in 2000.

Thomas Bourhill Johnston (Bourhill was his mother's maiden name) goes down in O's folklore as the club's greatest all-time player, as voted by the fans in a 1999 Millennium poll, gaining over twenty per cent of all votes cast. Born at Loanhead, five miles from Edinburgh, on 18 August 1927, he was tagged 'The Happy Wanderer', playing in every class of professional football with three Scottish clubs, one Welsh club and seven English clubs (in every division) with a career total of 237 League goals (268 including goals in cup competition) from 406 appearances. He still holds Orient's seasonal and aggregate goalscoring records. Johmston had a remarkable season in 1957/58, scoring 37 goals from 27 League and FA Cup matches. There was much talk of him breaking Dixie Dean's record of 60 goals, but unfortunately he was transferred to Blackburn Rovers for £15,000 – a move he later said that he regretted – netting a further 8 goals with the Ewood Park club. He ended the season as the League's top goalscorer with 43 League goals and a single FA Cup goal. Dean's record would surely have been broken had he stayed in Leyton. In one spell with O's, Johnston hit 67 goals in 82 matches. Today, Tommy has wandered to Sanctuary Point, New South Wales, Australia. Pride of place on his mantlepiece are two tankards presented by the club – one for his goalscoring feats and the second in celebration of his seventieth birthday back in August 1997. In 1991 he was diagnosed with bowel cancer, but has bravely battled through and today still follows O's fortunes with keen interest. His scoring record is impressive to say the least: in 1955/56 he scored 8 goals from 15 appearances; 1956/57 yielded 27 from 42; 1957/58 gave 35 from 30; 1958/59 brought 10 from 14; in 1959/60 he notched 25 from 39 and in his final season, 1960/61, he grabbed 16 from 40 games played. On top of this total of 121 goals in 180 League games for Orient, he scored 2 goal in 7 games in the FA Cup, but failed to find the net in his 3 League Cup appearances for the club.

As well as his remarkable heading ability, Johnston also had a powerful left foot shot. In this picture he is shooting past Clary Williams in the Grimsby Town goal on 21 December 1957. This was a game in which he notched up yet another hat-trick for Orient in their 5-1 win. In all he notched up four hat-tricks and on one occasion scored four goals in a match.

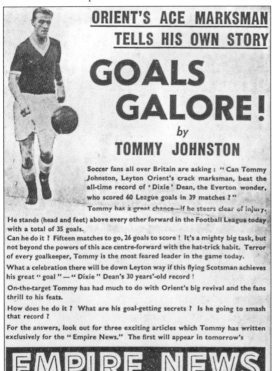

Would Johnston break Dixie Dean's goalscoring record? The *Empire News* ran this report.

Four
The Ups and Downs
of the 1960s

With the likes of Lord Bernard Delfont and brother Leslie Grade on the board, many local and international stars were seen at Orient matches during the late 1950s and early 1960s, including Cliff Richard, Shirley Bassey, Arthur Askey and Pat Boone. American singer Boone sent the O's players special hats after one of his visits in 1960. Photographed here with their hats on are, from left to right: Joe Elwood, Tommy Johnston, Dave Groombridge, Eddie Brown, Stan Charlton, Ron Foster, Les Gore (manager), Ken Facey, Terry McDonald, Sid Bishop, Nick Collins (coach), Alan Eagles and Dennis Sorrell.

The programme cover for the visit of Sheffield Wednesday in a FA Cup fifth round tie on 18 February 1961. O's 0-2 defeat was witnessed by a crowd of 31,000.

Stan Charlton, goalie Frank George and Ken Facey are clearing their lines against Wednesday. This was Facey's last season as a first-teamer. A wonderful servant, he still stands second only behind Tommy Johnston on O's all-time goal scoring chart with 79 senior goals from 323 matches. He is also Orient's penalty king, with 23 conversions from 27 spot kicks between 1952 and 1961.

The biggest match in Orient's League history to date took place on 28 April 1962, the last day of the 1961/62 season. The O's and Sunderland were level on points in second and third position, Liverpool having already been established as champions. Orient were at home to Bury, while Sunderland travelled to third-from-bottom Swansea. The tension was almost unbearable for the 21,617 crowd. Thankfully, late replacement Malcolm Graham scored twice to secure a 2-0 win and Sunderland could only manage a 1-1 draw – Orient were promoted! The scenes were unforgettable. This page shows the first goal and some of the celebrations.

Captain Stanley Charlton is chaired from the pitch by jubilant fans.

O's players Eddie Lewis, Dave Dunmore, Sid Bishop, Norman Deeley, Bill Robertson and Stanley Charlton take the applause from the crowd. Dunmore was brilliant that season with 22 League goals.

The hero of that tense final game, Malcolm Graham, celebrates after the match with a glass of champagne. Graham recalls director Leslie Grade calling him over in the dressing room after the match and saying, 'Malcolm thank you, my dreams have come true. If I can give you anything, anything just tell me now.' To this offer Graham replied 'Yes, another glass of champagne'. As Graham recently said to the author from his home in Barnsley, 'I was young and naive in those days. I should have said "Mr Grade – my bond". And you know what? Grade would have paid it, he was dead serious.'

The architects of promotion, manager Johnny Carey (*right*) with his assistant Les Gore. The final positions in Division Two in 1961/62 were:

	P	W	D	L	F	A	Pts
Liverpool	42	27	8	7	99	43	62
Leyton Orient	42	22	10	10	69	40	54
Sunderland	42	22	9	11	85	50	53

This is the team that took Orient up to Division One for the first time only in their history. From left to right, back row: Lucas, Bishop, Robertson, Lea, Lewis. Front row: Deeley, Gibbs, Charlton, Dunmore, Graham, McDonald.

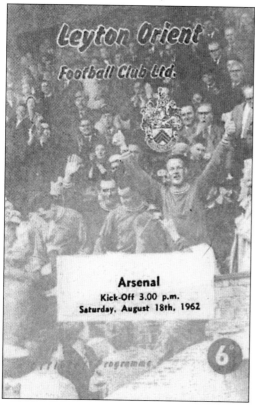

This is the programme cover for the first match in Division One, versus Arsenal, on 18 August 1962. O's lost the encounter 1-2 in front of a crowd of 26,300. Derek Gibbs hit Orient's first goal in the top flight.

This is the team line-up for the League Cup tie against Chester on 17 October 1962. The game was unusual in several respects. Not only did Orient rack up an impressive 9-2 victory, but Malcolm Graham and Norman Deeley both scored hat-tricks. It was also during this game that eighteen-year-old Roger Wedge made his only senior appearance for the O's. Eight months earlier, Wedge had been called up for the FA Cup tie versus Burnley when Phil White had flu. It was the latter who finally played, however, and Wedge had to be content with watching the match from the dugout. Today, Wedge runs a sports tavern in Brighton, and still thinks of what might have been.

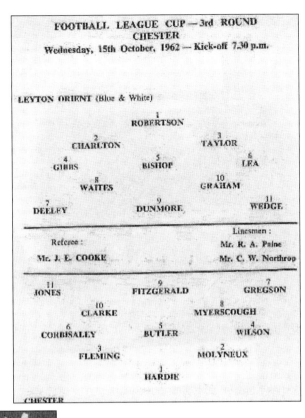

FOOTBALL. LEAGUE CUP — 3rd ROUND
CHESTER
Wednesday, 15th October, 1962 — Kick-off 7.30 p.m.

LEYTON ORIENT (Blue & White)

1
ROBERTSON

2   3
CHARLTON   TAYLOR

4   5   6
GIBBS   BISHOP   LEA

8   10
WAITES   GRAHAM

7   9   11
DEELEY   DUNMORE   WEDGE

Referee :   Linesmen :
Mr. J. E. COOKE   Mr. R. A. Paine
                                   Mr. C. W. Northrop

11   9   7
JONES   FITZGERALD   GREGSON

10   8
CLARKE   MYERSCOUGH

6   5   4
CORBISALEY   BUTLER   WILSON

3   2
FLEMING   MOLYNEUX

1
HARDIE

CHESTER

Leyton Orient
Football Club Ltd.

F.A. CUP. 4th Round
LEYTON ORIENT
v.
WEST HAM
Saturday, 25th January, 1964   Kick-off 3 p.m.

Official 6ᵈ Programme

This is the programme cover for the game that attracted Brisbane Road's record attendance. A massive crowd of 34,345 turned up for FA Cup clash with West Ham United on 25 January 1964. Norman Deeley scored in the opening minute, but Peter Brabrook equalised for the Hammers. West Ham won the replay, played in front of 35,383 fans, 3-0.

55

This is Orient's line-up for the match against Norwich City on 6 February 1965. From left to right, back row: Metchick, Hollow, Nelson, Pinner, Harris, Gregory. Front row: Worrell, Price, Dunmore, Sorrell, Musgrove. Orient lost the encounter 3-2. This was the final game for goalkeeper Mike Pinner who, having made 83 senior appearances, moved to Distillery. By contrast, it was the League debut of twenty-three-year-old Jeffrey Harris, who had joined O's from Enfield Town. He made just 14 appearances before joining Romford in the Southern League. This 1964/65 season was also to be the last for thirty-one-year-old David Dunmore, who had netted 58 senior goals from 168 appearances, as he returned to his native York in June 1965. The picture features a new badge introduced by Dave Sexton, although this blue and white striped design only lasted for six months.

Paul Went runs out for his League debut against Preston North End on 4 September 1965. Aged just 15 years and 327 days, he is the youngest player ever to appear for Orient in the League. Went went on to enjoy a long playing career of 474 League appearances and 42 goals. The youngest known player to play in the League was Albert Geldard at 15 years and 156 days for Bradford Park Avenue on 16 September 1929. Later in life, Went became O's shortest-lived managerial appointment (see page 90).

LEYTON ORIENT SUPPORTERS CLUB

A SPECIAL MEETING

WILL BE HELD
IN THE MAIN SEATING STAND
AT
LEYTON STADIUM

on SUNDAY 20th November, 1966, at 11 a.m.

DIRECTORS AND OFFICIALS OF THE LEYTON ORIENT
FOOTBALL CLUB WILL BE IN ATTENDANCE
including Mr. Arthur Page and Mr. Dick Graham

ALL THOSE INTERESTED IN LEYTON ORIENT
WHETHER MEMBERS OF SUPPORTERS CLUB
OR NOT ARE INVITED

ADMISSION BY THIS TICKET ONLY

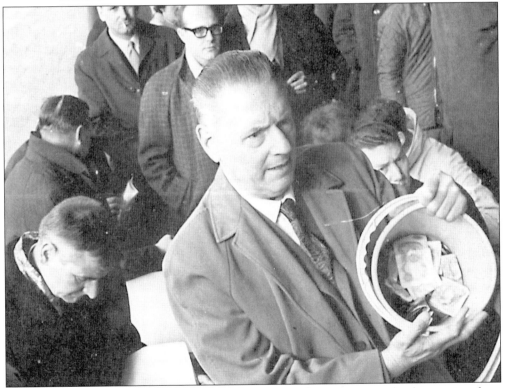

Top: With O's dropping into the Third Division and average crowds plummeting from 13,257 in 1960 to 5,972 in 1965, the directors announced on 29 October 1966 that the club were £100,000 in the red, losing £1,500 each week and close to liquidation. On 20 November 1966, the famous 'pass the bucket' meeting was held at Brisbane Road. On hand to lead the fight were chairman-elect Arthur Page and director Harry Zussman. Thousands of pounds were raised by this method, while former directors Lord Bernard Delfont and his brother Leslie Grade each gave £10,000. At the end of the season young Paul Went was sold to Fulham for £30,000 and the O's were saved.

The team for the 1966/67 Division Three campaign. During October 1966, due to the financial crisis, Les Gore, along with coach David Clark and groundsman Jack Tonner, were fired by boss Graham. Gore had been a wonderful servant to the club for over sixteen years in various capacities. He was appointed scout with Charlton Athletic, a position he held until his death at Buckhurst Hill, Essex on 21 January 1991, aged seventy-seven. From left to right, back row: Bradbury, Snedden, Forsyth, Ferry, Rouse, Willis, Bowtell, Whitehouse, Went, -?-, Street, Wigg, Clarke (trainer). Middle row: Goodgame, Jenkins, Smith, O'Brien, Carter, Allen, Metchick, Le Flem, Jones, Bailey, Woodward, Sorrell, Cowan (trialist). Front row: Rofe, Brisley, Price, Les Gore (coach), Eddie Heath (youth manager), Dick Graham (manager), Mr C. Bent-Marshall (director), Arthur Page (chairman), Frank Harris (director), George Hicks (secretary), Marshall Hicks (assistant secretary), Johnny Hartburn (pools promoter), Commons, Vancoeverden. Cliff Holton is missing from this picture.

Five
The Great FA Cup
Runs of the 1970s

The Division Three championship was won by Orient when Mark Lazarus headed home the winner on 25 April 1970 against Shrewsbury Town. Captain Terry Mancini is pictured here lifting the trophy two days later with Mickey Bullock, who hit 19 goals during the season.

The Leyton Orient squad with the Third Division Championship Cup, 1970/71. From left to right, back row: Barrie Fairbrother, Phil Manning, Terry Brisley, Bobby Arber, Steve Bowtell, Ray Goddard, Dennis Rofe, Peter Brabrook, Eddie Presland, Mick Jones. Middle row: Brian Blower (pools promoter), George Hick (secretary), Ian Filby, Gerry Sullivan, Malcolm Filby, Paul Harris, Tommy Taylor, Bobby Moss, Dave Harper, Peter Allen, Peter Angell, (trainer), Charlie Simpson (physiotherapist), Len Cheesewright (youth manager). Front row: Dickie Plume, Mark Lazarus, Barry Dyson, Terry Mancini (captain), Arthur Page (chairman), Frank Harris (director), Reg Briggs (director), Jimmy Bloomfield (manager), Terry Parmenter, Mickey Bullock, Martin Binks. The O's had finished two points clear of second-placed Luton Town and eight points ahead of Bristol Rovers in third position. In the 46 League games played during the season, Orient won 25, drew 12 and lost 9, scoring 67 goals and conceding 36.

This is the cover of the programme for the match that was staged to celebrate promotion on Monday 4 May 1970 at Brisbane Road versus Roma of Italy. Orient lost the game 1-3 in front of over 8,000 fans.

Orient returned to Division Two with a bang on 15 August 1970, beating Sheffield United 3-1 in front of 10,584 spectators. The day belonged to thirty-two-year-old, Stepney-born Mark Lazarus, who scored two glorious goals. A colourful character, Lazarus would do a lap of honour after every goal he scored. He recorded 136 League goals from 441(3) matches during his career. Nowadays he runs a family transport business in Romford.

Twenty-year-old Ian Bowyer, a £25,000 record signing from Manchester City, scoring the first goal of his home debut hat-trick in a 4-1 win over Cardiff City on 21 August 1971. By the end of the season he was the O's top-scorer with 17 senior goals. Bowyer stayed with Orient for three seasons, scoring 23 goals from 75(3) appearances before a £40,000 move to Nottingham Forest in October 1973. Nowadays he is assistant manager with Birmingham City.

After the sudden departure of Jimmy Bloomfield, Orient appointed thirty-nine-year-old George Petchey as manager in July 1971. Petchey, a wing-half with over 400 League appearances to his credit, had spent his entire football career with London clubs West Ham United, QPR and Crystal Palace. He had been coach at Palace when they were promoted to Division One. As a manager, Petchey advocated the push-and-run style of play and was instrumental in bringing many fine young players through the ranks during his six-year stay with Orient. In the 254 games played under Petchey, Orient won 74, drew 89 and lost 91 games, scoring 257 and conceding 294 goals.

Nineteen-year-old Tommy Taylor, on his way to First Division West Ham United for £80,000 plus Peter Bennett, says farewell and good luck to newly appointed secretary John Falltrick in 1971.

Orient faced a star-studded side Chelsea in a home FA Cup tie on 26 February 1972. After 36 minutes, O's were 0-2 down to goals from Webb and Osgood and looked dead and buried. Then, on the stroke of half-time, Phil Hoadley hit a stunning 30-yard goal to lift the spirits. Within three minutes of the restart, the scores were level: Allen's long pass into the Blues' penalty area saw both Webb and Bonetti hesitate, the ball spinning off Webb's foot into the path of Bullock, who side-footed into an empty net in a home fifth round FA Cup tie.

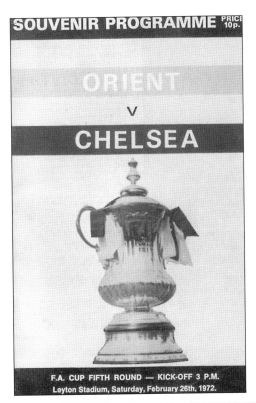

In the last minute of the match, with the score still at 2-2, Bullock controlled a clearance and touched the ball to Walley, who sent a wonderful ball down the centre for Bowyer and Fairbrother to chase. Bonetti came running out of his goal and the ball broke to Fairbrother, who chipped it into the net past a helpless and grounded Webb. At the final whistle, O's fans swarmed onto the pitch to celebrate a famous victory.

Another shot of Fairbrother's great last-minute goal. *Insert*: Millions of people saw the final result on BBC's *Match of the Day* that evening.

Orient team group, 1972/73. From left to right, back row: Bullock, Bennett, Fairbrother, Hoadley, O'Shaughnessey, Goddard, Bowtell, Harris, Riddick, Arber, Bowyer, Third row: Allen, Dyson, Johnson, Filby, Kinnear, Fulton, Lewis, Rofe, Downing, Brisley. Second row: Les Cheesewright (chief scout), Peter Angell (trainer), Mr R.S. Briggs (vice-chairman), Mr F.F. Harris (director), Mr M. Page (director), George Petchey (manager), Mr Arthur E. Page (chairman), Mr Harry S. Zussman (director), John Fulltrick (secretary), Ron Gilson (assistant secretary), Arthur Rowe (general advisor), Ernie Shepherd (physiotherapist), Brian Blower (commercial manager), Miss Janet Smith (backroom staff). Front row: Tutu, Bragg, Drummy, Sullivan, Botham, Fisher, Woodward, Smeulders, Grealish, Cunningham, Robinson, Hibbs, Roeder, White. This side finished in fifteenth place in Division Two. Barrie Fairbrother was the top scorer with 11 goals.

In the home match with Millwall on 6 April 1974, this 'goal' was disallowed after consultation between the officials. In the photograph, Barrie Fairbrother (number 9 on socks) scores O's controversial 'goal', with Terry Brisley having been pushed into the net by a Lions player. Although not interfering with play, Brisley was ruled offside by the referee and Gerry Queen's celebrations proved premature. This decision meant that Orient only took a single point from the match, which ended 1-1, and was, in the author's opinion, the turning point that cost O's promotion.

In the end, it all boiled down to Orient having to win their final League match, against Aston Villa, on 3 May 1974 to pip Carlisle United for a place in the old First Division. What an atmosphere there was, with 29,766 in the ground to witness the deciding game. Unsurprisingly, the match was very tense affair and at half-time the score stood at 0-0. Early in the second half, Villa winger Brian Little ran into the box and was brought down by a late Phil Hoadley tackle, upon which the referee promptly awarded a penalty. This action shot shows Ray Graydon blasting home the spot-kick.

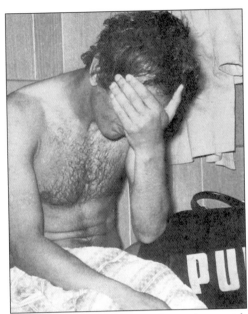

Two goals were now needed for promotion. Bullock lobbed home an equalizer, then, with seconds remaining, hit a tremendous shot that Villa 'keeper Coombes somehow managed to turn over the crossbar. At the final whistle O's had failed by a single goal and everyone was devastated. This picture shows Barrie Fairbrother and Ricky Heppolette sitting crying in the dressing room, reflecting on what might have been.

Barrie Fairbrother is voted Player of the Year for 1973/74, the first season in which the award was made. Only one player has won this trophy more than once – Paul Heald in 1990/91 and 1991/92 – and only five forwards have won in the twenty-seven years that the award has been running.

A cartoon of some of the O's squad for the 1973/74 season, drawn by supporter George Keeling. From left to right, top row: Ian Bowyer, Terry Brisley, Tom Walley, Ricky Heppolette. Middle row: Peter Allen, Bobby Arber, Ray Goddard, Gerry Queen. Bottom row: Derrick Downing, Peter Bennett, Phil Hoadley, Paul Harris. In many cases, former players return to their first club as coach, trainer or even manager. How many return as a chiropodist? Paul Harris did just that, being appointed as Leyton Orient's foot specialist in 1998, having made 110(2) appearances and scoring 4 goals for O's in the 1970s.

The first ever book on the history of the club was launched at the match versus Norwich City on 26 October 1974 with help of two 'Oriental' ladies. Over 8,000 copies were sold over the following months. In this photograph, publisher John Maxwell presents O's chairman, Brian Winston with a special leather-bound, gold-embossed limited edition. He is seen with the authors, Alan Ravenhill (left) and club historian Neilson N. Kaufman (right).

Phil Hoadley and Bobby Fisher tussle with Stuart Pearson as Tom Walley heads clear.

Phil Hoadley and Bobby Fisher tussle with Manchester United's Stuart Pearson while Tom Walley heads clear in a match played at Old Trafford on 14 December 1974. Orient gained a credible 0-0 draw in this match at the Red Devil's famous stadium. The 1974/75 season did nothing to bring the crowds back to Brisbane Road, however, O's playing out 12 goal-less draws and scoring just 28 League goals all season.

Orient became London five-a-side champions at the Wembley Indoor Arena in May 1975, beating QPR (Stan Bowles and all) 6-1 in the ITV televised final. Pictured with cup are, from left to right: Phil Hoadley, Peter Allen, Gary Hibbs (reserve), Derek Possee (with trophy), John Jackson (behind Lady Aitken) and Terry Brisley.

Two of the great legends of East London football, Orient's Laurie Cunningham and Bobby Moore (playing for Fulham) at Brisbane Road on 28 February 1976. Moore played over 660 League matches with both West Ham and Fulham. He died of bowel cancer on 24 February 1993. Cunningham was born in Archway, London on 8 March 1956 and was arguably one of the most gifted players ever to wear an O's shirt. His first appearance for Orient came for the Colts at Gillingham in April 1972. He went on to wear the number 7 shirt for three seasons, making 82(4) senior appearances and scoring 16 goals (he played 216 games at all levels for the club, scoring 51 goals). Cunningham was transferred to West Bromwich Albion in March 1977 for £110,000 plus Joe Mayo and Allan Glover (who were valued at over £100,000). Of Jamaican descent, he became the first black player to be capped for his country for the England under-21 side, scoring with a downward header on his international debut. He gained 6 full England caps between 1979 and 1982. Cunningham left West Brom, after 81(5) appearances and 21 goals, for Real Madrid in June 1979 for £995,000, and scored on his debut at the Bernabeau. He later won a FA Cup winner's medal when he played for Wimbledon in their famous win over Liverpool in 1988. Sadly, he died in a car accident in Spain in the early hours of Saturday 15 June 1989. Laurie Cuningham was recently voted joint third with Peter Allen in Orient's all-time greatest player poll, receiving five per cent of the votes. The abilities of the East End's own 'Black Pearl' will remain in the memories of all O's supporters who were privileged enough to see him in action.

The main picture shows part designers of O's current badge, Clive M Brown and Mark Hodges. From left to right: O's first badge of the 1940s taken from the Borough of Leyton crest. The badge used on the programme cover between 1966 to 1970. Clive M. Brown's original 1976 design for O's current badge. The final design of the current badge, completed by then chairman Brian B. Winston.

Orient have had five different badges on their shirts since a badge was first worn in the late 1940s. The initial badge was introduced to the fans on a programme cover on 28 September 1946 for the visit of Crystal Palace, when the club announced its change of name to Leyton Orient Football Club. This design was worn on the shirts during the following few seasons and was based on the arms of the Borough of Leyton, showing three Chevronel Gules with a Lion passant. On the bottom, a wreath supported a crozier of gold with the Latin motto *Ministrando Dignitas*, meaning 'Dignity through service'. The colours of the crest were red and gold and, although not used on the shirts from 1954/55, remained as the official club badge until 1965 when the Borough of Leyton was incorporated in to the new Waltham Forest Administration. During the mid-1960s, O's replaced the Latin motto by incorporating the name 'Leyton Orient FC'. In 1965, new manager Dave Sexton designed a small blue and white striped badge, which was dropped when Sexton departed in December 1965. From August 1966, Orient changed their official shirt colours from blue to red and introduced two new badges. On the shirts was sported an oval badge with the colours of blue, white and yellow. It is said that O's director and shipping magnate Reg Briggs suggested the coloured badge, which was comprised of the official colours of shipping company P&O Group – this being the company that took over the Orient Shipping Company, whom O's had been named after some seventy-three years previously. This badge was worn up to 1969/70 season. The badge shown on the front cover of the programme was that of a single wyvern (a heralidic animal which resembles a dragon except it has no hindquarters, its rear being like a serpent with a barbed tail). O's then introduced a new motif of a single female griffin in white, which was first used for the visit of Sheffield United on 15 August 1970. The mythical griffin creature is symbolic of vigilance and strength and is said to guard against all danger and keep evil spirits away. During August 1976, Orient announced a competition for the design of a new club badge. On 27 December 1976, the final version of the badge was introduced. The winning design was based on two different suggestions submitted by Clive M. Brown and Mark Hodges. The final design was completed by chairman Brian Winston and sent to the London-based College of Arms.

Above: The current badge, with the name Leyton Orient, was incorporated from 1 July 1987, after the club reverted back to the name Leyton Orient FC.

Chairman Brian Winston with some supporters at the very first 'Meet the Chairman' evening, held at the Supporters Club in 1975. Born in Whitechapel, London on 19 September 1937, Winston was appointed as director in 1972, taking over as chairman in May 1974 from Arthur Page. Under his leadership, O's remained for Second Division outfit for many years. He left the club in 1985, but was asked to return a year later to broker a financial package to save the club from liquidation with Tony Wood as new owner. The deal was done and the club saved. In November 1986, Winston finally left the club. Today, he still follows O's fortunes with keen interest.

Orient team group, August 1976. From left to right, back row: David Payne, Mike Everett, Glenn Roeder, Peter Bennett, John Jackson, Nigel Gray, Gerry Queen, Bill Roffey, Ricky Heppolette. Third row: Tony Grealish, Gary Hibbs, Bobby Fisher, Peter Allen, Billy Hurley, John Smeulders, John Holmes, Phil Hoadley, Doug Allder, Laurie Cunningham, Derek Possee, John Chiedozie. Second row: Peter Angell (coach), Robert Hunt (groundsman), Carol Stokes (office assistant), Mike Blake (assistant secretary), Peter Barnes (secretary), George Petchey (manager), Brian Winston (chairman), Harry Zussman (director), Adrian Harding (director), Max Page (director), Brian Blower (commercial manager), Arthur Rowe (advisor), Terry Long (coach). Front row: Chris Henney, Stephen Johnson, Terry Glynn, Tunji Banjo, Billy Porter, Colin Johnson, Henry Hughton, Kevin Godfrey, Terry Emanuel, Tony Scanes. This season will be remembered for the excellent run to the final of the Anglo-Scottish Cup and Allan Glover's vital last goal of the season against Hull City to secure Second Division survival.

The programme cover for the Anglo-Scottish Cup final first leg on 7 December 1976 at Brisbane Road. The competition was first introduced in 1975/76 for English and Scottish clubs by invitation of the English and Scottish governing bodies. Orient faced Nottingham Forest in the two-legged final after an excellent run. This was O's first final in any major cup competition.

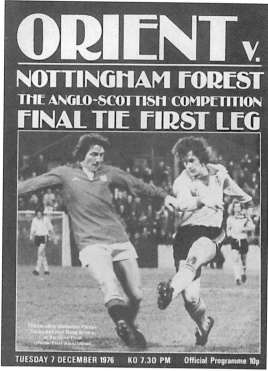

Derek Possee eludes full-back Frank Clark to head O's equaliser in the first leg, which finished as a 1-1 draw. Sadly, Orient lost the second-leg 3-0 at the City Ground on the following Wednesday, thereby losing the final 1-4 on aggregate. Still, it was a great overall performance in the competition, with four exciting wins over Scottish opposition that included Partick Thistle and Aberdeen.

On 17 May 1977, Orient went into the final match of then season, against Hull City, needing a point to avoid relegation to the Third Division. Allan Glover fired O's into a 1-0 lead, but on 73 minutes goalkeeper Jackson made a rare error. Hull's Paul Haigh hopefully chipped goalwards and, agonizingly, the ball bounced off the turf and slipped through Jackson's hands into the net. O's nervously held on, however, to keep their Division Two status and the 8,400 crowd went wild with delight.

Arthur Page, the man who saved the club from closure in 1966, died on 6 July 1977. Born in Bethnal Green on 14 January 1910, he was appointed as a director of the club in 1947. Page left Orient in 1951, only to return seven years later at the invitation of Harry Zussman. He was made O's life president after his eventual retirement on 3 May 1974.

Joe Mayo heading Orient into the lead during their visit to White Hart Lane for the game against Tottenham on 25 February 1978. This was only the tenth League meeting between the clubs and the Second Division fixture, which attracted a crowd of 32,869, ended 1-1.

Peter Charles Allen became the holder of O's League appearance record – breaking the forty-five-year-old record of Arthur Wood – on the occasion of the game against Sunderland on 13 March 1976. He went on to became the only Orient player to make over 400 League appearances for the club on 26 April 1977 against Southampton and ended up with total of 424(8) appearances and 27 goals for the O's. He made a total of 473/9 senior appearances with 29 goals with O's. His record is unlikely ever to be broken with the advent of the Bosman ruling. Allen was a hard but fair player and will be remembered for his remarkable versatility, loyalty, leadership and sportsmanship. A true professional, today he works as a solicitor at his Sussex practice. Allen also holds the record for playing the most seasons for the O's – thirteen in all. This is the programme cover for Peter Allen's testimonial match against West Ham United on 27 October 1975

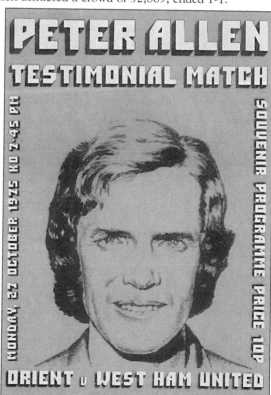

Julian Lloyd Webber presents O's chairman Brian Winston with a special gold disc of his hit LP *Variations* at the start of the match versus Leicester City on 30 September 1978. The background to this scene was that he had wanted his brother, Andrew Lloyd Webber, to write a cello piece for several years. Andrew kept stalling so they made a bet that should Orient get the required point over Hull City to avoid relegation for the final match of the 1976/77 season, Andrew would write for his younger brother. O's achieved their goal in a nail-biting affair and Julian won the bet. He had supported the O's since he was a boy of eleven, watching them in the old First Division, his first hero being Dave Dunmore. In later seasons he admired the goalscoring ability of Peter Kitchen: 'One of my greatest O's moments was watching us knock out Chelsea in the cup at Stamford Bridge back in 1978. Those Kitchen goals were absolutely brilliant.' As boys, the two brothers watched many O's matches together, but Andrews's patience wore thin. Julian, however, still watches Orient as much as he can and has said: 'I am a season ticket holder and an Executive Club member and I do think things are financially secure at the club since Barry Hearn has taken over.'

THE O's FA CUP SEMI-FINALISTS 1977-78

The Orient squad, 1977/78. From left to right, back row: John Chiedozie, Allan Glover, Tunji Banjo, Peter Kitchen, Derek Clarke. Middle row: Bill Roffey, Joe Mayo, John Jackson, John Smeulders, Nigel Gray, Peter Bennett. Front row: Bobby Fisher, Glenn Roeder, Peter Angell (assistant manager), Phil Hoadley (captain), Jimmy Bloomfield (manager), David Payne, Tony Grealish. Kevin Godfrey was away on reserve team duty when this picture was taken. During this season, O's had a brilliant FA Cup run all the way to the semi-finals with some thrilling displays. The 7 FA Cup goals from Peter Kitchen were superb and such prowess had not been seen by O's fans since the days of Johnston. Indeed, 'Kitch' goes down as arguably one of the better strikers to play for O's and ranks alongside the likes of McFadden, Crawford, Neary, Facey and Johnston.

Peter Kitchen smashes home a goal against Norwich in the 1978 FA Cup home tie.

A remarkable last minute save by John Jackson against Chelsea earned O's a replay at Stamford Bridge in the fifth round. In the second match, held nine days after the initial encounter, the opening goal was a true Kitchen classic. The O's forward ran onto a pass from young Kevin Godfrey, sprinted past Ron Harris, skipped over Mickey Droy's lunging tackle, dummied Ian Brittain and shot past the advancing Peter Bonetti – a fabulous effort!

Bonetti was beaten again as Kitchen put Orient 2-0 up and the O's went through to the quarter-finals with a famous 2-1 victory. The insert shows the players celebrating in the dressing room after the match.

Orient had reached the FA Cup quarter-finals for the first time and put on a battling display with a goal-less draw at First Division Middlesborough's Ayresome Park. Back at Brisbane Road, Kitchen, nicknamed the 'Goal Gourmet', hit the opener in the replay on 14 March 1978 – a goal described by the player himself as the best he ever scored for O's.

Joe Mayo's shot finds the net against Boro and the O's are 2-0 ahead. They eventually won the tie 2-1 and went on to face Arsenal in the semi-final stage.

Kitchen and Mayo celebrate their goals, which took Orient to the FA Cup semi-finals, with a cup of tea.

The O's are on the attack. Arsenal goalie Pat Jennings punches clear from Mayo with Kitchen in attendance. Eighteen-year-old Tunji Banjo (inset) came on as a substitute in the semi-final for, remarkably, his only cup appearance that season. He is pictured here with trainer Peter Angell. Banjo played a total of just 22(9) matches for O's with 2 goals, yet went on to win 7 international caps for Nigeria. He later described his 20 minutes on the field in the semi-final as the highlight of his career.

F.A. CUP
Semi-final
At Stamford Bridge

Official
Programme
30p.

CHELSEA
FOOTBALL & ATHLETIC CO. LTD № 750
Football Association Cup Semi-Final
ARSENAL v. ORIENT
SATURDAY APRIL 8th 1978
Kick off 3 p.m.
You are advised to be in position by 2.15 p.m.
NORTH TERRACE STANDING
(Brittania Entrance C)
£2.00 inc. VAT
This ticket is issued subject to the Rules and Regulations of the Football Association and the Football League, and is allotted on the distinct condition that no holder thereof shall sell or transfer same for a larger price than appears on the face hereof. In the event of any breach of this condition, the Chelsea Football Club Ltd. reserves the right to cancel this ticket and retain the money paid therefore on allotment.
TO BE RETAINED

ORIENT v ARSENAL
Saturday, April 8th, 1978 Kick-Off 3p.m.

Above: O's first FA Cup semi-final was played against First Division Arsenal at Chelsea's Stamford Bridge. The team surprisingly included the experienced Derek Clarke (at the expense of Kevin Godfrey) for his only FA Cup match of the season and young Tunji Banjo as reserve. The match attracted a crowd of 49,698, who handed over gate receipts of £147,225. *Middle:* Match ticket. *Right:* Captain Phil Hoadley walks onto the Stamford Bridge pitch with the Cockney Pearly king and queen.

81

The second deflected goal of the semi-final – Malcolm MacDonald's shot ricochets off Roffey (3), sending John Jackson the wrong way. In the end, Orient went down 0-3. The dream of a Wembley FA Cup final appearance had ended, yet it was still a very proud day for all O's fans.

With all the interest of the FA Cup run, some forgot about the League and O's had to win at Cardiff City on 9 May 1978 to avoid the drop into Division Three. Here, Kitchen squeezes between two City defenders to hit the winner. This vital strike was his 29th senior goal of the season – by far the best return for an Orient player since the days of Tommy Johnston in the 1950s.

Loyal coach and assistant manager Peter Frank Angell collapsed and died during a squad training session in Epping Forest on 18 July 1979, aged forty-seven. Angell had enjoyed a wonderful playing career with 450 senior appearances for QPR between 1955 and 1965. He had been coach of O's championship winning side of 1969/70 and had taken charge of the Orient team that reached the FA Cup semi-finals in 1978, when boss Bloomfield was hospitalised for long periods.

DREAM DEBUT FOR TONY GREALISH
Nottingham Forest's Miah Dennehy looks on as Tony lets fly at the Forest goal. Below; Congratulations from team mates after his 20th minute goal puts "O's" in the lead.

Anthony 'Paddy' Grealish had a wonderful career, winning 7 Eire caps whilst with Orient and 44 caps in total. The all-action midfielder made 192(3) senior appearances and scored 10 goals for the O's. Tony joined Luton Town for £150,000 in August 1979 and made a career total of over 600 senior matches. Nowadays, he works in the scrap-metal business. He is pictured here scoring on his full debut versus Nottingham Forest on 30 November 1974.

'Butter fingers' – John Jackson with O's director Harry Zussman at a Christmas party in December 1978. Jackson joined Orient in October 1973 for a bargain £25,000 from Crystal Palace after 346 League appearances for the Eagles (including a run of 222 consecutive games). He is ranked second behind Arthur Wood as Orient's greatest ever goalkeeper and made 256 senior appearances for O's, including 210 consecutive League appearances between 1974 and 1979. At the age of thirty-seven, Jackson left Orient and joined his old boss George Petchey at Millwall for £7,500 in August 1979. Jackson, who made a total of 656 League appearances, was later coach at Brighton with Petchey, leaving the South Coast club in May 1998.

Six
Centenary to
Promotion in the 1980s

Alec Stepney, Altrincham's goalkeeper, saves Ralph Coates' shot, but Joe Mayo follows up to score Orient's 200th FA Cup goal on 9 January 1980 at Brisbane Road.

In a shock move, Stanley Bowles joined Orient in July 1980. He is seen here being welcomed by physiotherapist Bill Songhurst (left) and secretary Peter Barnes. Bowles was manager Bloomfield's biggest name signing and came from Nottingham Forest for £90,000. When disciplinarian Ken Knighton arrived as manager in 1981, Bowles was the first to leave. He joined Brentford, having made 50 senior appearances and scored 7 goals for Orient. Songhurst was with O's for over sixteen years before leaving to spend more time in his own clinic in 1992. Barnes came from Crystal Palace in 1973 and moved to Tottenham Hotpsur in 1980. He was appointed as the secretary of the White Hart Lane club in 1987.

Orient splashed out a club record £150,000 in November 1980 for former England wingman Peter Taylor from Tottenham Hotspur. In this photograph, he is being welcomed by manager Jimmy Bloomfield. Taylor stayed for three seasons making 55(7) senior appearances. Later, he became England under-21 manager and was boss at both Gillingham and Premiership side Leicester City. In October 2000 he was appointed as the acting manager of the England national side following the resignation of Kevin Keegan.

Sponsors have played an important part in the financial survival for the clubs in the lower divisions of the Football League for the last two decades. Shirt sponsorship was first allowed in January 1981 and O's became the very first London club to sign a sponsorship deal, when Essex-based Everard Ovenden Paper Co paid to have EO papers displayed on the kit. The company was owned by former O's director, fifty-four-year-old Neville Ovenden. He later became the controlling shareholder of the club, in November 1982, but resigned with his son, Michael, six years later. Ovenden died in Nazing, Essex on 5 February 1994. As a mark of respect, the players observed a minute's silence before the match versus Bradford City on 12 February. In this photograph, chairman Brian Winston and manager Jimmy Bloomfield hold the new EO sponsored shirt; Ovenden is in the background.

The end of a League career – midfielder Steve Parsons crys with pain after breaking his leg at Grimsby Town on 14 February 1981. Despite an effort to return, he never played League football again. The Hammersmith-born player had joined Orient from Wimbledon in March 1980 for £42,000.

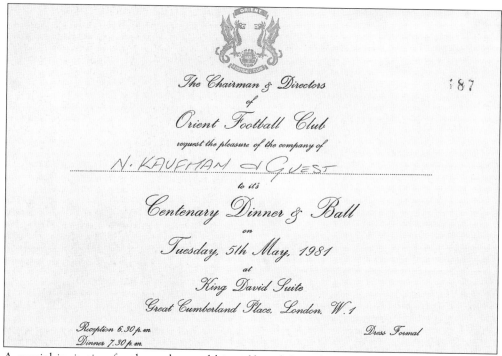

The Chairman & Directors
of
Orient Football Club
request the pleasure of the company of

N. KAUFMAN & GUEST

to its

Centenary Dinner & Ball

on

Tuesday, 5th May, 1981

at

King David Suite
Great Cumberland Place, London, W.1

Reception 6.30 p.m.
Dinner 7.30 p.m.

Dress Formal

187

A special invitation for the author and his girlfriend, Ingrid Austin, to O's centenary dinner and ball at the King David Suite of the Great Cumberland Hotel, London on 5 May 1981.

In a presentation in May 1981, Ted Croker, secretary of the Football League, presented an illuminated address to Orient chairman Brian Winston to mark the club's centenary, in a presentation at the dinner ball.

Harry Zussman, the cherubic charmer, died of a heart attack at his Shoreditch offices on Friday 10 July 1981. Born in Hanbury Street, Brick Lane, London on 24 June 1919, he was appointed as O's chairman in 1949. He remained on the board for over thirty-two years – right up to his death. His friendly, permanently smiling face is missed by everyone and it was because of him that Orient became known as London's friendliest and most welcoming football club. This picture of Zussman was taken at the O's centenary dinner, two months before his death.

John Okay Chiedozie came to England as a thirteen-year-old from Owerri, Nigeria in 1973 to avoid the civil war in that country. Initially at West Ham, he joined Orient as an apprentice in July 1976. He made his Second Division debut against Millwall on 8 March 1977, after the sale of Laurie Cunningham. Chiedozie was transferred to First Division Notts County for an O's club record of £600,000 in August 1981 after 146(14) senior appearances and 23 goals. He won 7 Nigerian international caps while with Orient. 'Chidders' retired in 1989 and nowadays runs a company that hires out bouncy castles for parties from his home in the New Forest. He is pictured here scoring at Sheffield Wednesday on 25 October 1980 and posing in the Nigerian Green Eagles tracksuit after winning his first cap against Tunisia in 1980.

Paul Went came from being O's youngest player ever to make a first team debut, to becoming manager of the club – albeit for just twenty-one days until his sacking by chairman Brian Winston on 12 October 1981, shortly after the morning training session had been completed. There seem to be no hard feelings, as Went and Winston, along with Paul's wife, Wendy, met for a drink at Went's pub in Essex two months after his dismissal. Went's record at Orient reads as follows: played 9, won 1, drew 1, lost 7; goals for 3, goals against 15. Went first took charge of the team as acting manager for the first match of the 1981/82 season at Derby County on 29 August. He was appointed as manager on 22 September and sacked on Monday 12 October. The five matches of which he was in full control were all lost, with 0 goals scored and 10 conceded.

Opposite above: Unsurprisingly, Orient were bottom of Division Two after Paul Went's short and disasterous spell as manager. The men appointed to lead the fightback were thirty-seven-year-old Ken Knighton, who was appointed manager in October 1981, and thirty-eight-year-old Frank Clark, who joined as his assistant in November. Their track record was good as together they had taken Sunderland up to Division One in 1979/80. Clark spent eleven years with O's, being appointed managing director in November 1986. His stay culminated with promotion to Division Three via the play-offs in June 1989, to become only the fourth manager to lead an O's team to promotion. Clark replaced Brian Clough at Forest on 12 May 1993. Nowadays, he works as a radio and TV commentator. Clark's record, from May 1983 to May 1991, reads as follows: played 372, won 145, drawn 88, lost 139; goals for 547 and goals against 511.

Jimmy Bloomfield died in April 1983 after a long illness, aged forty-nine. This photograph shows the players paying silent respect for his passing at Oxford United on 9 April. Bloomfield had two spells as manager with Orient. He originally joined the club as player-manager on 8 March 1968, after 451 League appearances with Brentford, Arsenal, Birmingham City and Plymouth Argyle, and took O's to the Third Division championship in 1970. After a successful spell with Leicester City, he returned to Orient in September 1977, but was in and out of hospital during his later years in charge. He resigned in 1981, due to his ill-health and his unhappiness over the John Chiedozie transfer to Notts County. Bloomfield's record, from March 1968 to May 1971 and September 1977 to August 1981 reads as follows: played 316, won 102, drawn 106, lost 108; goals for 350, goals against 369.

Peter Kitchen is one of only eleven O's players to have bagged four goals in a League match. This feat was captured on camera on 21 April 1984 against Millwall. The last O's player to net four goals in a match was Steve Castle at Rochdale in May 1986.

Kevin Godfrey's most memorable day came on 23 September 1985 when his two goals gave O's a 2-0 victory over Tottenham Hotspur in a League Cup match at Brisbane Road. Unfortunately, O's lost 0-4 in the second leg to crash out 2-4 on aggregate. A winger, Godfrey stayed at Orient for eleven seasons and ended as O's fourth all-time goal scorer with 72 senior goals from 298(33) appearances. He joined Brentford in October 1988, scoring a further 17 goals from 92(27) appearances. Godfrey ended his career with non-League Yeading FC and is now a taxi driver.

After O's chairman Neville Ovenden had resigned due to ill health, he called in former owner Brian Winston to look at the books of the club. Winston found that the club was close to liquidation and brokered a deal with O's former O's Vice President Club member and director of a few months, Tony Wood. Wood is pictured here on 5 January 1975, having just received an OBE for his work as Honorary Consul to Rwanda, with members of the O's Vice Presidents Club, Brian Fredericks and Melvyn Plannar. This was the eventful day on which O's knocked West Brom out of the FA Cup.

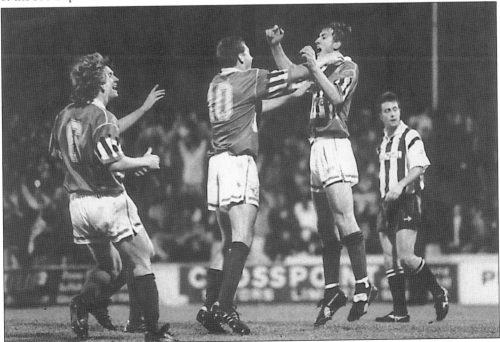

Greg Berry hits two goals past the West Bromwich Albion defence in a rousing 2-1 FA Cup victory, allowing Woods to celebrate his OBE in a right royal way.

Orient team group, 1986/87. From left to right, back row: Chris Jones, Steve Castle, Alan Comfort, Stephen John, Ian Jury. Third row: Pat Holland (youth manager), Colin Foster, John Cornwell, Robert Quinnell, Peter Wells, Dean Greygoose, Peter Mountford, Kevin Godfrey, Andy Sussex, Bill Songhurst (physiotherapist). Third row: Tommy Cunningham, Shaun Brooks, John Sitton, Frank Clark (manager), Lee Harvey, Paul Shinners, Kevin Hales, Kevin Dickenson. Front row: Kevin Nugent, Darren Went, Chris Snell, Warren Barton, Richard Mason, Mark Gribble, Barny Shorter, Hakan Hayrettin, Michael Gilbert, Ian Rawling. Orient finished the season in seventh position. Manager Frank Clark went to the board for permission to sign on Kevin Nugent and Warren Barton as apprentices, but was informed that, due to a lack of money, he could only sign one of them. Clark went for Nugent, even though he knew that seventeen-year-old Barton had excellent potential. Barton joined Leytonstone & Ilford, went on to Maidstone United, Wimbledon and then Newcastle United in August 1994 for £4 million. He was at that time the most expensive defender in British football and won a total of 3 England international caps. Nugent played for the O's for five seasons before his move to Plymouth in 1992.

The first issue of *Orientear* was launched in September 1986 to represent the many alternate views that the supporters held. The magazine has become an institution and in the days of super technology it has still managed to maintain its audience. It was first started by Steve Harris, and around four years ago Jamie Stripe became its editor. There are two other O's fanzines: *CheeryO's*, started in 1996 by Nick Madden, and *Pandemonium* (formerly *All Aboard the Wagon Train*) set up a few years ago by Matt Roper.

94

Kevin Campbell, who joined O's on loan from Arsenal, opens his account with a header at Crewe on 21 January 1989. His 9 goals from 16 appearances help Orient reach the play-off finals.

Mark Cooper proved the hero with two fine goals in the first leg against Scarborough on 21 May 1989, in front of 9,289 spectators. In this shot, Cooper, having scored the second goal with eight minutes remaining, is being hugged by Lee Harvey, with skipper John Sitton also in the picture. The second leg was a tough encounter, which the O's lost 0-1. Orient went through 2-1 on aggregate.

Lee Harvey scores O's opening goal, on the stroke of half-time, against Wrexham in the second leg of the play-off final in June 1989. Harvey breasted down a cross from Alan Comfort and twisted a defender before shooting past goalkeeper Salmon to put Orient into a 1-0 lead. However, within two minutes of the restart, a Jon Bowden header pulled the Welsh side level. The first leg at Wrexham on Tuesday 30 May 1989 had been a goal-less affair, with O's having much of the play. The decider at Brisbane Road was watched by a crowd of 13,355.

The match was seemingly heading for extra time – and the possibility of the Welshmen going through on the away goals rule – when, on 82 minutes, Steve Baker fed Lee Harvey through on the right; Harvey crossed the ball and Mark Cooper hooked it into the goal from twelve yards. After the final whistle the excitement was reminiscent of the promotion scenes of 1956, 1962 and 1970.

Mark Cooper is mobbed by elated fans as he leaves the field.

Manager Frank Clark receives applause from the players and fans for guiding O's to promotion.

The players celebrate in the dressing room away from the crowds. From left to right, top: Kevin Dickenson (on ground), Alan Hull, Paul Ward, Terry Howard, Lee Harvey, John Sitton, Steve Baker, Kevin Hales. Front: Steve Castle, Paul Heald, Keith Day, Mark Cooper. Alan Comfort is missing from the celebrations, having been whisked away to Hackney Marshes to get a helicopter to Heathrow so he could catch a plane in order to be married at 5.30 p.m. in Ireland!

The Wrexham match was to be Alan Comfort's final performance for Orient, as he was transferred to Middlesbrough during the summer for £175,000. Comfort, who ended as top scorer with 19 senior goals, can be compared with another great wingman, Owen Williams, who had also left London for Middlesbrough, some sixty-five years earlier. Like Williams, there was a buzz around the ground whenever he received the ball. Sadly, Comfort's career was cut short at Newcastle on 4 November 1989. In trying to retrieve a ball he fell and twisted his knee. His leg was put in plaster but, despite three operations, his football career was over. He decided to enter into the clergy and said at the time, 'I would love to return to East London – there is a job to be done there. It is where I played most of my football. When I got badly injured a lot of people just disappeared, but not Frank Clark at Orient. He always kept in touch.' Nowadays, the Revd Alan Comfort is vicar of St Stephens church in Buckhurst Hill, Essex and is also the chaplain of Leyton Orient Football Club. He was recently voted second behind Tommy Johnston as O's all-time greatest player, receiving eleven per cent of all votes cast.

Seven

The 1990s, Wembley and the New Millennium

The programme cover for the game against Bury on Saturday 14 April 1990. This was Orient's 1,000th Football League match at Brisbane Road. Unfortunately, they lost this historic encounter 2-3. O's League record at Brisbane Road, from 28 August 1937 to 6 May 2000, reads as follows: played 1,232, won 585, drawn 329, lost 318; goals for 1,982, goals against 1,714.

Midfielder Chris Bart-Williams with new manager Peter Eustace and managing director Frank Clark. Bart-Williams made his full debut for Orient at the age of 16 years and 232 days against Tranmere Rovers on 2 February 1991. Born in Freetown, Sierre Leone on 18 June 1974, he made 34(2) League appearances for the O's before a £350,000 move to Sheffield Wednesday (including £70,000 for goalie Chris Turner) on 21 November 1991. The total deal, following his 60th appearance for the Hillsborough club, was worth some £575,000. Bart-Williams made 95(29) League appearances for Wednesday before a £2.5 million transfer to Nottingham Forest on 1 July 1995.

Kevin Nugent sees off First Division Oldham Athletic with O's fourth goal in extra time of a replay at Brisbane Road on 15 January 1992. Nugent, after five seasons of service for Orient, was sold in March 1992 to Plymouth Argyle for £275,000, having netted 16 senior goals in the season. Nowadays he is still finding the net for Cardiff City.

Ricky Otto fires home from close range in O's game against Bournemouth on 17 October 1992. Orient's 1-0 win over the Cherries meant that they jumped from fifth to top position in Division Two (thus leading their division for the first time in twenty-one seasons). Ricky Otto, with his unusual hairstyle tied up in a bun, showed great ability and pace down the left wing and the mystique of his past soon made him a cult figure. The emergence of Otto was one of the major highlights at Orient during the early 1990s. Otto moved to Southend United for £100,000 on 9 July 1993.

Twenty-two-year-old New Zealander Christopher Vincent Zoricich came to London to continue his studies after graduating at Auckland University. 'Zoro', as he was nicknamed, joined O's in 1991 and was a very useful squad member for three seasons. He won 3 New Zealand caps whilst with Orient, in World Cup qualifying matches against Fiji and Vanuatu (twice). During 1993 the classy defender was refused a work permit, even after a petition of over 1,000 O's supporters names. He returned home after making 59(12) senior appearances and scoring 1 goal. Recently he was located in Australia, playing with Newcastle United, and nowadays captains the New Zealand national side, having gained over 40 full caps.

The story of Robert Taylor makes interesting reading. He came to Orient on loan from Norwich City on 28 March 1991. After ten days and three appearances as substitute, with one spectacular goal at Crewe, he suddenly had to be rushed back to Norwich for an emergency appendix operation. After a two-month lay-off, he found himself without a club and was planning to go back to college to study physical education. He phoned O's boss Peter Eustace to arrange to collect some boots he had left at Orient. After a long chat, Eustace offered him a trial. Taylor impressed so much that he was offered an eighteen-month contract. In 1992/93 he hit 18 League goals and in March moved to Brentford for £100,000. Taylor has performed credibly over the years, with some big money transfers – £600,000 to Gillingham in August 1998 and £1.5 million to Manchester City on 26 November 1999. This forward with a deft touch and an eye for goal has scored well over 100 goals in his professional career. If it weren't for a chance call some eight years ago, his talent would have been lost to League football. In May 2000 he scored a vital goal to take Manchester City back up to the Premiership. In August 2000 he moved to Wolves for £1.55 million.

Andy Jones dives to head home Orient's fifth goal in a thrilling FA Cup match at Dagenham & Redbridge on 14 November 1992. A capacity 5,300 crowd witnessed what was described by the two managers, John Still and Peter Eustace, as the best game that they had ever seen. The epic encounter finished 5-4 in Orient's favour – but football was the real winner.

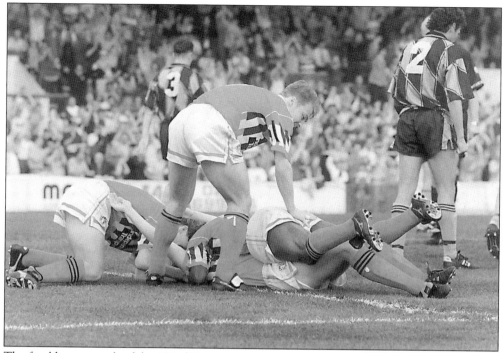

The final home match of the 1992/93 season was a 4-2 win over Bradford City; Ricky Otto and Lee Harvey are celebrating a Robert Taylor goal in true style.

A record 3,000 crowd was at Tiverton on 12 November 1994. The O's had not won away for over a year and the locals were expecting an FA Cup shock after taking the lead on 12 minutes. Orient had other ideas, however, and this image shows Andy Gray celebrating his equaliser on 33 minutes. After this strike, the wall behind the goal collapsed and several O's fans obtained minor injuries from falling onto mud and grass on the edge of the pitch. The first on the scene was O's winger Danny Carter. He stated 'Had the fans been crushed onto concrete it could have been a very serious situation.' Then came Gray, Cockerill and Bogie to help the fans up. The match eventually restarted with O's winning 3-1. It was later ascertained that the wall behind that goal had only been built the Friday before the match.

Photographer Dave Winter captures the dangerous scene. The wall has collapsed and Danny Carter (11) and Glenn Cockerill are helping the O's fans.

After the sacking of boss Peter Eustace in April 1994, assistant manager Chris Turner and youth coach John Sitton took over for the game at Huddersfield Town on 9 April 1994. The following season they were officially appointed as joint managers – it proved to be one of the worst campaigns in O's history, both on and off the field. Orient finished bottom of Division Three with just 6 wins all season, and the club was in a desperate financial position, only being saved from liquidation by its new owner Barry Hearn. After yet another home defeat, by Brentford on 17 April 1995, both men were sacked. One of the most bizarre decisions made by Sitton was the dismissal of long-serving crowd favourite Terry Howard.

Terry Howard, cult hero and club stalwart, dubbed by O's fans as 'Oooh', is sensationally sacked by boss John Sitton at half-time in the match versus Blackpool on Tuesday 7 February 1995, after eight years of loyal service and 376(6) senior appearances for Orient. The photograph shows Howard left sitting in the dressing room, somewhat bemused, with the note by his side. *Insert*: John Sitton.

Orient have never been blessed with prolific goal scorers. However, during the early 1990s, there were two marksmen who scored over 100 senior goals between them – Mark Cooper and Colin West – and who finished fourteenth and seventeenth respectively on O's all-time goal scoring list. Nowadays, Cooper is with Gravesend & Northfleet and West is assistant manager at Hartlepool with Chris Turner. This shot shows Mark Cooper and Colin West celebrating Cooper's goal against Cardiff City on 18 December 1993.

The final chapter in O's 114-year history seemed to have been written when Barry Sillkman, on behalf of pop star Rod Stewart and then local businessman Phil Wallace, pulled out of takeover deals. Then came the announcement for which every O's fan had been waiting. The club had been saved by Debden-born Barry Hearn, the famous boxing and snooker impresario, who bought it from Tony Wood during early March 1995. The first match Hearn attended as Orient's new owner was the Auto Windscreens semi-final against Birmingham City on 13 March 1995.

The programme cover for the home leg of the Auto Windscreens semi-final. Orient went down in the first game at St Andrews 1-0 in front of 24,002 spectators. O's lost the second leg 2-3, so it was City who went to Wembley.

New manager Pat Holland with Barry Hearn and Darren Purse. Holland was appointed as manager on 27 April 1995. The Poplar-born thirty-nine-year-old had spent his entire playing career with West Ham United, making 271(25) senior appearances and scoring 32 goals before injury ended his career in January 1981. He joined O's as a player in 1983, but was only a non-playing substitute at Wimbledon in the FA Cup during November of that year. After a number of seasons on O's coaching staff, he joined Spurs as youth coach in 1988 and was appointed reserve coach during 1992. His reign at Orient lasted 63 League matches and he was sacked on 28 October 1996. After a short coaching spell with QPR, he was appointed assistant manager at Millwall under Billy Bonds, but left after five months to rejoin Spurs' coaching staff.

After forty-two away League matches without victory, O's laid to rest their abysmal two-year run. They had last won at Hull City on 30 October 1993 and the drought finally came to an end on 12 September 1995, when they triumphed at Northampton Town. The magic moment came in the last minute, when Ian Hendon looped over a cross, Shaun Brooks volleyed back a clearance and Alex Ingelthorpe lunged in for the winning touch, making the final score 2-1. This photograph shows captain Dominic Naylor celebrating as Caldwell and Kelly embrace. Over 700 delirious fans floated back down the M1, with chairman Barry Hearn lining up the beers. He had forgotten the champagne, but stated 'This was marvellous. It was like our European Cup final and great for the fans ... all the players were magnificent.'

Roger Edmund Stanislaus and Barry Hearn at a drugs inquiry hearing. Stanislaus became the first British footballer to be banned from football for taking prohibited performance-enhancing substances. He was given a twelve-month ban on 1 February 1996. Stanislaus had been caught when tested after a match at Barnet on 25 November 1995 – the first time that Orient had been chosen for random testing in two years.

The 1995/96 season was to be the last for the popular and talented thirty-eight-year-old midfielder Glenn Cockerill, one of eight players released in May 1996. After the Sitton and Turner administration had been dismissed, he had acted as caretaker manager for the match at Bristol Rovers on 22 April 1995. Later he was with Fulham and Brentford. In July 1998, Cockerill became assistant manager with Bashley FC. Cockerill played a total of 771(49) senior matches and scored 95 goals in a League career that spanned some twenty-two years.

An enthusiastic 5,055 fans saw a makeshift Orient team take on the full Welsh national side for their warm-up match before facing San Marino in the World Cup. With a side comprised of mainly youth team members and trialists, O's defeated the star-studded Welsh team – which included Ryan Giggs, Mark Hughes, Dean Saunders, John Hartson, Barry Horne and Neville Southall – 2-1.

O's took the lead on 15 minutes through a Lee Shearer header. Twelve minutes from time the Welsh equalised through Robinson. O's still had a sting in their tail, however, and following a Tello run down the right, Baker hooked the ball back for Peter Garland to scramble home the winner.

Leyton Orient FC, 1996/97. From left to right, back row: David Chapman, Ian Hendon, Mark Warren, Alan McCarthy, Dave Hanson, Alex Ingelthorpe, Peter Garland. Middle row: Steve Shorey (chief scout), Terry Spurgeon (kit man), Dave Martin, Colin West, Peter Caldwell, Luke Weaver, Les Sealey, Lee Shearer, Andy Arnott. Front row: Dominic Naylor, Martin Ling, Justin Channing, Alvin Martin, Tommy Cuningham (assistant manager), Pat Holland (manager), Tony Kelly, Joe Baker, Sammy Winston, Sammy Ayorinde, Paul Brush (director of coaching/youth manager), Tony Flynn (physiotherapist). This season was one for unusual records. During 1996/97, O's had five golden oldies on their books whose ages totalled some 200 years. These veterans, who had played some 46(1) senior matches for O's between them, were: Alvin Martin (38), Les Sealey (39), Peter Shilton (47), Chris Whyte (36) and Ray Wilkins (40). The season saw no fewer than forty players used in the League and five goalkeepers featured – the youngest being a seventeen-year-old named Luke Weaver. By November 1996, both Holland and Cunningham had departed.

Following Holland's departure, it was forty-five-year-old former O' Tommy Taylor who got the nod, coming home to a club that he had first joined as a ten-year-old. Taylor had taken Cambridge United to second spot in the table, but his contract only ran to that December. He turned down the chance to manage Cardiff City saying, 'I'll walk down the M11 for this O's job'. That seemed to swing it and Taylor was appointed on 7 November 1996. Taylor is pictured here with Barry Hearn in the background. Taylor's record, including the 1999/2000 season, reads as follows: played 170, won 61, drew 49, lost 60; goals for 216, goals against 203.

Peter Shilton MBE, OBE, was born in Leicester on 18 September 1949 and became a footballing legend. At the age of 47 years and 72 days he made his League debut for the O's at home to Cardiff City on 30 November 1996. In doing so, he became the oldest player to play in the League for Orient. Shilton achieved a wonderful milestone on 22 December, making his 1,000th Football League appearance, thus becoming the only man to achieve such a feat, in a 2-0 win over Brighton – keeping his 333th clean sheet. Shilton played 1,390 League and cup matches in his career. He holds the record for caps won by a British player, with 125 between 1970 and 1990, with 90 clean sheets. His one goal came at Southampton in October 1967, when a long punt from his area took a freak bounce and cleared an embarrassed Campbell Forsyth. At his final League match, against Wigan, he was aged 47 years and 124 days. After a spell in Hong Kong, he was more recently goalkeeping coach with Middlesbrough. Like Bradman's test average of 99.94 and the 25 heavyweight title defences by boxer Joe Louis, Shilton's appearance record will probably stand for many decades.

Shilton runs out onto the red carpet treatment to a fanfare from the band of the Coldstream Guards. The 7,944 fans and players gave him a wonderful reception. His arrival on the pitch was shown around the world via BBC and CNN.

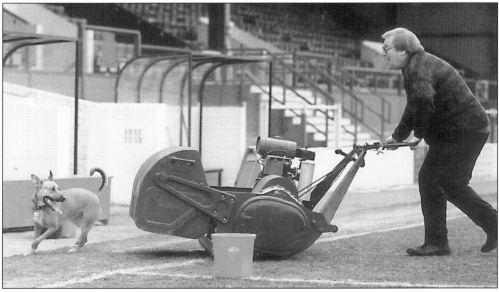

Orient's groundsman Charlie Hasler took over on 11 August 1977. He was won numerous awards, culminating in the grand prize during 1995/95, when he scooped the Wilkinson Sword groundsman of the year trophy. Quite remarkably, at the time of his award the club had no workable sprinkler or irrigation system. In 1996/97 he won the Third Division pitch of the year award and over the past few seasons has consistently been runner-up. This is a wonderful record for a man who has been associated with the club for over twenty-five years and who turned down the opportunity to work on the famous Wembley turf to stay with his beloved O's.

During the summer of 1996, break contractors remove over 20,000 tons of rubble from the Coronation Garden southern end of the stadium to make way for a new stand.

The match at Brighton on 8 March 1997 proved quite a remarkable affair. It had just about everything that is exciting, good and bad about football – eight goals, umpteen chances, many bookings, a controversial sending off (of Mark Warren), a pitch invasion, a last minute penalty and three O's players attacked on the field of play by a number of idiotic Brighton 'supporters'. This photograph shows Scott McGleish and other Orient players being attacked by hooligans.

The story of eighteen-year-old goalkeeper Luke Weaver is a remarkable one. After playing just 10 senior matches for O's, he was signed by Peter Reid at Sunderland for an initial fee of £250,000. If some remarkable sell-on and appearance clauses had come into play, the deal could have been worth between £850,000 and £1million. As it turned out, however, Weaver could only manage a handful of reserves appearances during his two years in the North East. He then joined Carlisle United on a free transfer on 26 August 1999. There was a twist to the tale though, as, after the disappointment of not receiving a larger slice of the proposed deal, O's got the original £250,000 on his departure from the Stadium of Light – but it appears that Sunderland were the ones who got the raw deal.

Goalie Paul Hyde signed full-time from Leicester City in March 1997 after a good spell of 141 appearances with Wycombe Wanderers. Tragedy struck at Exeter City on 31 January 1998, when this terrible tackle from City's John Williams resulted in Hyde breaking his leg in three different places. As the goalie cried out in pain, the ball broke free and the home side scored. The extent of Paul Hyde's injuries were such that he could never play League football again and was forced to retire. Orient gave him a testimonial on 29 March 1999 against West Ham United. Nowadays, he coaches O's goalkeepers on a part-time basis and, more recently, has played for Dover Athletic.

A number of songs have played an important part of football club histories through the years. West Ham's *I'm Forever Blowing Bubbles*, Liverpool's *You're Never Walk Alone*, *The Liquidator* at Leeds United, the *Theme from Z Cars* at Everton and Charlton's *Red Red Robins* being famous examples. For over thirty years, O's have had their own tune – *Tijuana Taxi*. The song, by Herb Alpert and the Tijuana Brass, was first played to lead O's players onto the field on 10 August 1968 for the Division Three clash with Rotherham United. The playing of the tune was the brainchild of then DJ Keith Simpson. After first hearing the tune on his mother-in-law's LP *Going Places*, he found the melody bouncy and catchy. He asked boss Jimmy Bloomfield what he thought, since O's were looking for a signature tune. Bloomfield thought it ideal and the tune was adopted. Simpson wrote in the programme for the Rotherham match, 'Listen out for Orient's new catchy theme tune – Herb Alpert's swinging version of *Tijuana Taxi*. This record will introduce the team every time they take the field and the club hopes it will become the signal for a really rousing cheer by Orient supporters.' *Tijuana Taxi* was written by guitar player Ervan 'Bud' Coleman. He was an A&M recording artist and a member of the group Baja Marimba Band. The words were by Johnny Flamingo. It was produced by Herb Alpert and Jerry Moss in 1965. This photograph shows the man who brought *Tijuane Taxi* to Brisbane Road, Keith Simpson, with the original LP in front of the O's newly built South Stand in August 1999.

Original music sheet cover and words by Johnny Flamingo with a special message from Herb Alpert, which was sent to the author in 2000.

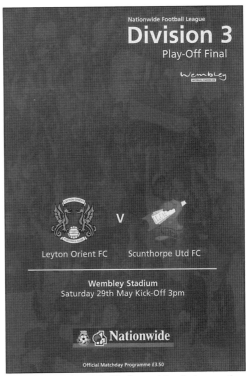

Above, left: 1999 play-off semi-final hero Scott Barrett (centre), with Hicks and Inglethorpe (on top), Beall, Lockwood and Walschaerts. The game against Rotherham in Yorkshire seemed set to enter extra time when the home team was awarded a free kick thirty yards from the goal. Roscoe's superb kick looked destined to curl into the net, but somehow Orient 'keeper Scott Barrett scrambled across his goal and at full stretch finger tipped the ball around the post to send the game into extra time. The tight match went into a penalty shoot-out and Barrett came out on top again with two wonderful saves. It was left to Matthew Lockwood to coolly slot home to take O's through to a Wembley play-off final against Scunthorpe United. *Above right and below:* Play-off final programme and match ticket for the game at Wembley on 29 May 1999 versus Scunthorpe United.

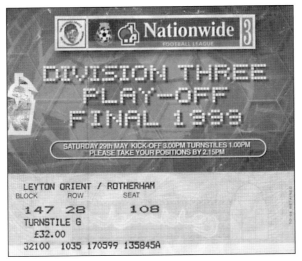

Manager Tommy Taylor leads the Orient players on to the Wembley pitch.

The O's players go into a huddle before kick-off.

A Steve Watts shot is scrambled away.

Another goal attempt, by Amara Simba, goes perilously close.

Ingelthorpe's shot in the final minutes is saved – Scunthorpe clung on to their slender 1-0 lead and were promoted.

Stan Charlton, one of the most popular players with the club since the Second World War, being presented with a tankard on the occasion of his seventieth birthday in August 1999 by Martin P. Smith (chairman of the O's International Supporters Club) and Dave Dodd (club director). A fine left-back with a unique sliding tackle, Charlton played for eleven seasons. This would have been longer had he not joined Arsenal in November 1955. He finally left the Orient in 1965, having made 408 senior appearances for the club. He was awarded a well-deserved testimonial for his loyal service in 1970.

The new South Stand, with 1,336 seats, is completed during August 1999. The Matchroom Stadium has a capacity of 13,494 with 9,204 seats. The 125-year lease agreement that the club signed with the Waltham Forest administration will allow further ground redevelopment at a later stage.

Leyton Orient team group, complete with the new strip of white shirts with red chevron (last worn by the club some fifty-five years previously), for the 1999/2000 season. From left to right, back row: Danny Curran, Andy Harris, Iseyden Christie, Wim Walschaerts, Roger Joseph, Alex Ingelthorpe, Matthew Lockwood, Kwame Ampadu. Middle row: Dean Smith (captain), Simon Clark, Stuart Hicks, Ashley Bayes, Scott Barrett, Barry Andrews, Joshua Low, Steve Watts, Tony Richards. Front row: Dave Morrison, Matthew Joseph, Joe Baker, Martin Ling, Billy Beall, Nicky Shorey, Johnny Martin, Scott Canham.

One of the bright lights in what was a very disappointing 1999/2000 season was the rise of eighteen-year-old, Romford-born Simon Downer. The central defender showed maturity beyond his years, which was rewarded with a professional contract on 1 October 1999. The £1million-rated player has already attracted scouts from Premiership clubs.

The French influence has certainly left its mark on English football in recent years, and Orient were one of the clubs to benefit. On 7 October 1998, thirty-seven-year-old former French international Amara Sylla Simba signed for O's after a successful career in France and with Mexican club Lyon. Just minutes after his debut, he became the darling of the Brisbane Road faithful with a headed goal against Exeter City. He was top scorer in 1998/99 with 11 senior goals. Senegal-born Simba did things with the ball seldom seen in Division Three. This accomplished striker moved to Kingstonian and scored their winning goal against Kettering in the FA Trophy final at Wembley in May 2000.

Ahmet Brkovic, a skilful and creative twenty-five-year-old Croatian midfielder, came to O's as a free agent in October 1999, signing a six-month contract on the 5 November 1999. He had met a Romford girl in Croatia and they decided to get married, settling in Essex. He started his career with his local side FC Dubrovnik and was with FC Varteks-Varazdin before arriving in England. Brko' signed a new one-year contract with Orient in July 2000.

Steve Watts joined O's in October 1998 from Fisher Athletic after winning a professional contract through a competition in the *Sun* newspaper to find O's a new striker. Watts admitted 'I saw details about the competition, but I was so nervous before the trial I almost threw up.' Watts, originally a printer by trade, is looking forward to a successful third season with the club.

Tough-tackling, twenty-eight-year-old Belgium player Wim Walschaerts joined O's from Second Division Belgian side KFC Tielen of Antwerp in July 1998, having previously played for Beerschot FC. He has quickly settled into the English style of play. Voted by both the *Fantastic O's* and *Cheery O's* fanzine as their player of the year for 1998/99, much is expected of this talented player.

Carl Griffith was born in Oswestry, Shropshire on 16 July 1971 and brought up at Forden, near Welshpool. He returned for his third spell with O's on 16 December 1999 for £80,000, a deal financed by chairman Barry Hearn. Griffith was originally transferred from Orient to Port Vale for £115,000 on 24 March 1999, much to everyone's surprise. At the end of January 2001 he was in joint thirteenth position, with 55 senior goals for the club. Could the 2000/2001 season see 'Griff' become only the tenth O's player to record over 20 League goals in a season?

Eighteen-year-old Kosovan refugee Niam Uka has shown great courage. On returning home from a two-year spell with the Partizan Club in Albania in September 1998 he found that everything had been destroyed and his parents and brother had disappeared. He had to escape to avoid being killed and lived for eight weeks in the mountains, often going for days without food or water, before walking two days to neighbouring Macadonia. Uka arrived in South Wales after spending five days on the back of a lorry travelling across Europe to escape the troubles. He was placed in a refugee asylum in North London with a little money, a T-shirt and a pair of football boots. The chap who ran the asylum notified the FA after seeing his skills in the backyard with a football. Now Uka has swopped the killing fields of the former Yugoslavia for the football field of Leyton Orient's Brisbane Road. Uka was taken under the wing of Players Agent Richard Cody, a friend of O's chairman Barry Hearn. The young Kosovan went to O's for a trial and assistant boss Paul Clark said of the youngster 'Judged on individual skill and technique, there's no better player of his age in the country.' Uka now lives with the Cody family in Hornchurch, Essex, resigned to the fact that his family are probably dead, but he is not giving up hope that the Red Cross may still find them alive. He made his O's reserve debut at Norwich City on Tuesday 7 December 1999, showing some wonderful pace and dribbling ability down the right wing. He impressed so much, he was offered a two-year professional contract the following day. His extraordinary journey was rewarded when he was on the bench for the final Division Three League fixture against York City on 6 May 2000, sitting with fellow foreigners Brkovic from Croatia and Walschaerts from Belgium. He made his debut versus West Ham in a Charity match ten days later. So impressed were they by his story and courage that the Fantastic O's e-mail group have taken Uka under their wing and sponsored him for the 2000/2001 season. There are high hopes that over the next few seasons Niam Uka will emulate some of the great O's youngsters of the past, like Cunningham and Chiedozie, and become a great player himself. Uka has said of his experiences, 'I didn't think I would make it here alive. Everything is still difficult – England is a new country for me. I am trying to look forward, but I won't forget.'

Paul Brush was quoted in the club programme after his full-time appointment during August 1996 that his aim was to see the young players progress into League football. Well, his dream certainly came to fruition during the 1999/2000 season with no fewer than eleven youth players making it into the first team or onto the bench – an O's record. Plaistow-born Brush had a wonderful career with West Ham, Crystal Palace and Southend United, playing over 300 senior matches. He also appeared in the BBC television programme *Fantasy League Football* as Basil Brush's boss. For the start of the 2000-2001 season Brush was appointed Youth Director.

Steve Castle, the tenacious midfielder, rejoined O's in July 2000 after being away for over eight years. He has proved to be a prolific scorer and it was hoped that he would improve on his ranking of seventh in O's all-time list of marksmen, having already amassed 67 senior goals from his previous two spells with the club. However, due to a number of serious injuries he managed just one substitute appearance, in the FA Cup, up to January 2001. Castle scored his 100th League goal whilst with Peterborough United in 1999. He is here seen celebrating after converting a penalty against West Ham United in the FA Cup on 10 January 1987.

Orient players line up at Wembley.

Fans and flags at Wembley.

More flags at Wembley.

Ampadu comforts captain Smith after the final whistle.

Leyton Orient team group, 2000/2001. From left to right, back row: Steve Castle, Brendan McElholm, Simon Downer, Matthew Lockwood, Wim Walschaerts, Neil Gough, Andrew Harris, Isyeden Christie. Middle row: David Parsons, David McGhee, Dean Smith (captain), Scott Barrett, Steve Watts, Ashley Bayes, Tony Richards, Ray Akontoh, Richard Garcia. Front row: Nicky Shorey, Chris Dorrian, Billy Beall, Ahmet Brkovic, Carl Griffiths, Jason Brissett, Jade Murray, John Martin. Not in photograph: Niam Uka, Matthew Joseph. The squad are pictured with the name of the new sponsor Matchroom Sports on their shirts, the eleventh sponsor since January 1981. the others have been EO Papers/Ovenden Papers, Taylor Walker, Leggett Freightways, Comet Roofing, Baman, Independent Transport, HEAT, Acclaim, Marchpole and Bravo TV.

Southend-born Matthew Lockwood, a left-sided wing-back, joined Orient on 7 August 1998 on a free transfer from Bristol Rovers, after making 66 senior appearances. Rovers' loss was undoubtedly Orient's gain. The twenty-four-year-old highly-rated player is now valued in the £1 million bracket, and could soon be Orient's highest value transfer since John Chiedozie went to Notts County for £6,000 in August 1981.

Born in Bethnal Green on 30 September 1972, this right wing back has proved to be a tenacious tackler and excellent at pushing forward. He was rewarded after some wonderful displays for the O's by becoming only the thirteenth player to gain full international recognition, when he was selected for Barbados against Guatemala in a World Cup match on 9 October 2000. He gained one further cap against the USA in November 2000.

A unique group of former Orient players, pictured at a recent players' reunion. The group had a staggering 2778/36 senior appearances for O's between them, and had scored 250 goals. From left to right, back row: Peter Allen, Mark Lazarus, Stan Charlton, Paul Shinners. Front row: Tommy Cunningham, Sid Bishop, Phil Hoadley, Bill Roffey, Revd. Alan Comfort, Michael Peter Kitchen.